flaminio gundy

Krakow

Where angels also take the tram

Krakow
Where angels also take the tram

By Flaminio Gundy

Kindle Direct Publishing, USA, 2023

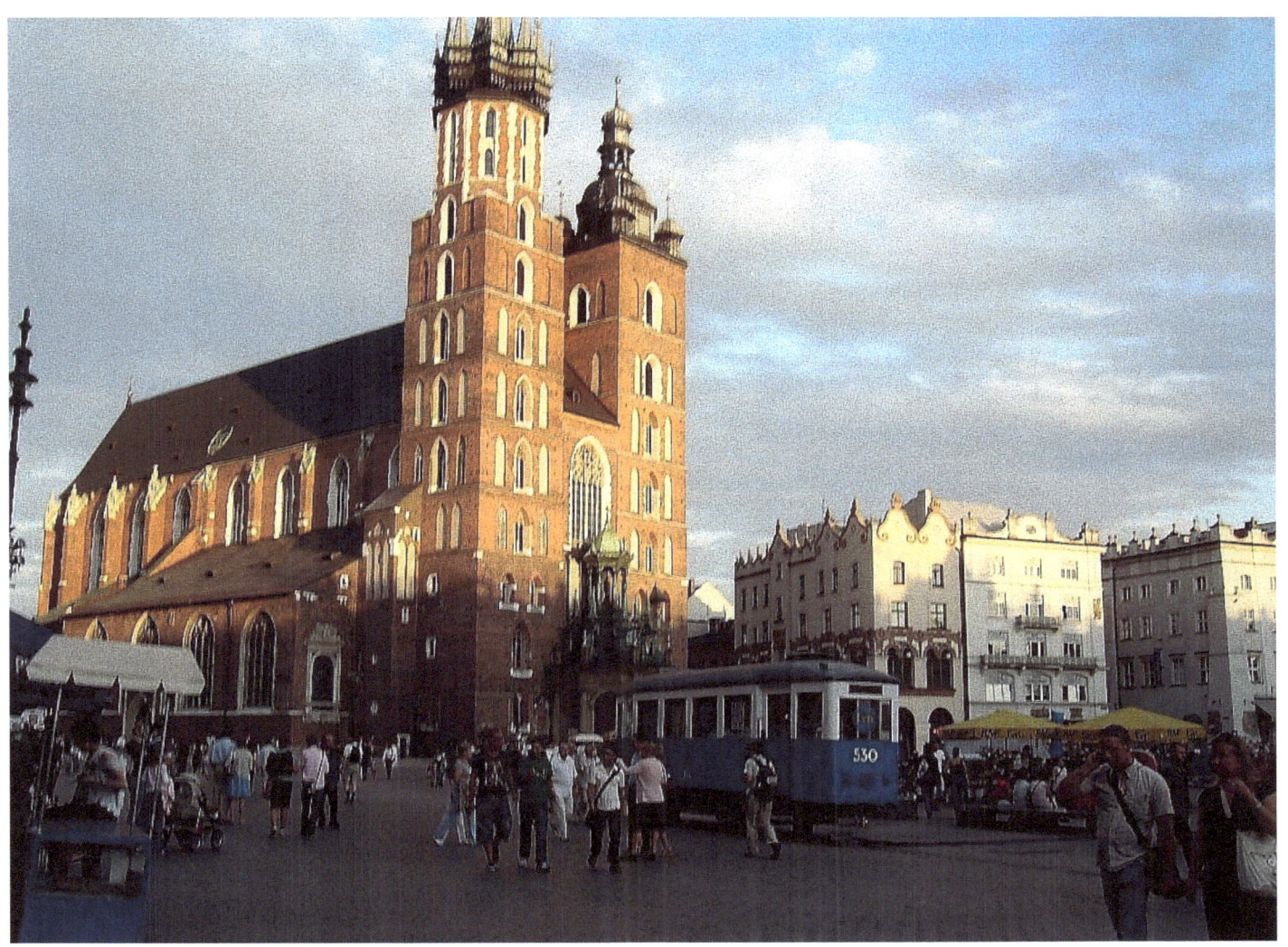

Zupa ziemniaczana, potato soup. Cut the potatoes into small cubes and cook with the onion cut into slices in a saucepan with a little butter. When the onion begins to color, add the canned sauerkraut, which are already semi-cooked and flavored with vinegar. Season for a couple of minutes, stirring and then cover with plenty of boiling broth of meat or vegetable. Cook for ten minutes. Sauté the smoked bacon in small cubes with a little butter and then add it to the soup. Cook for another ten minutes, adding more broth to taste. Finally, add a jar of yogurt, bring to a boil and serve.

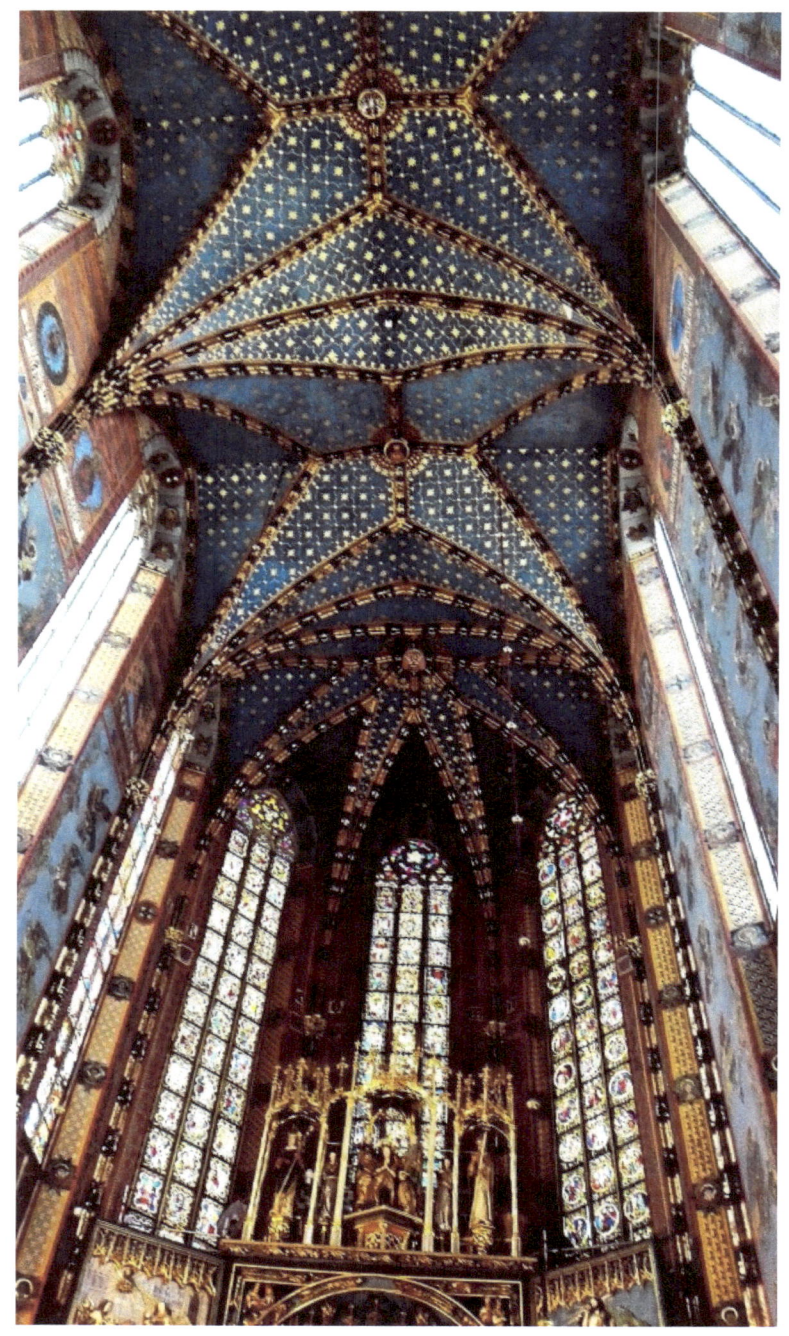

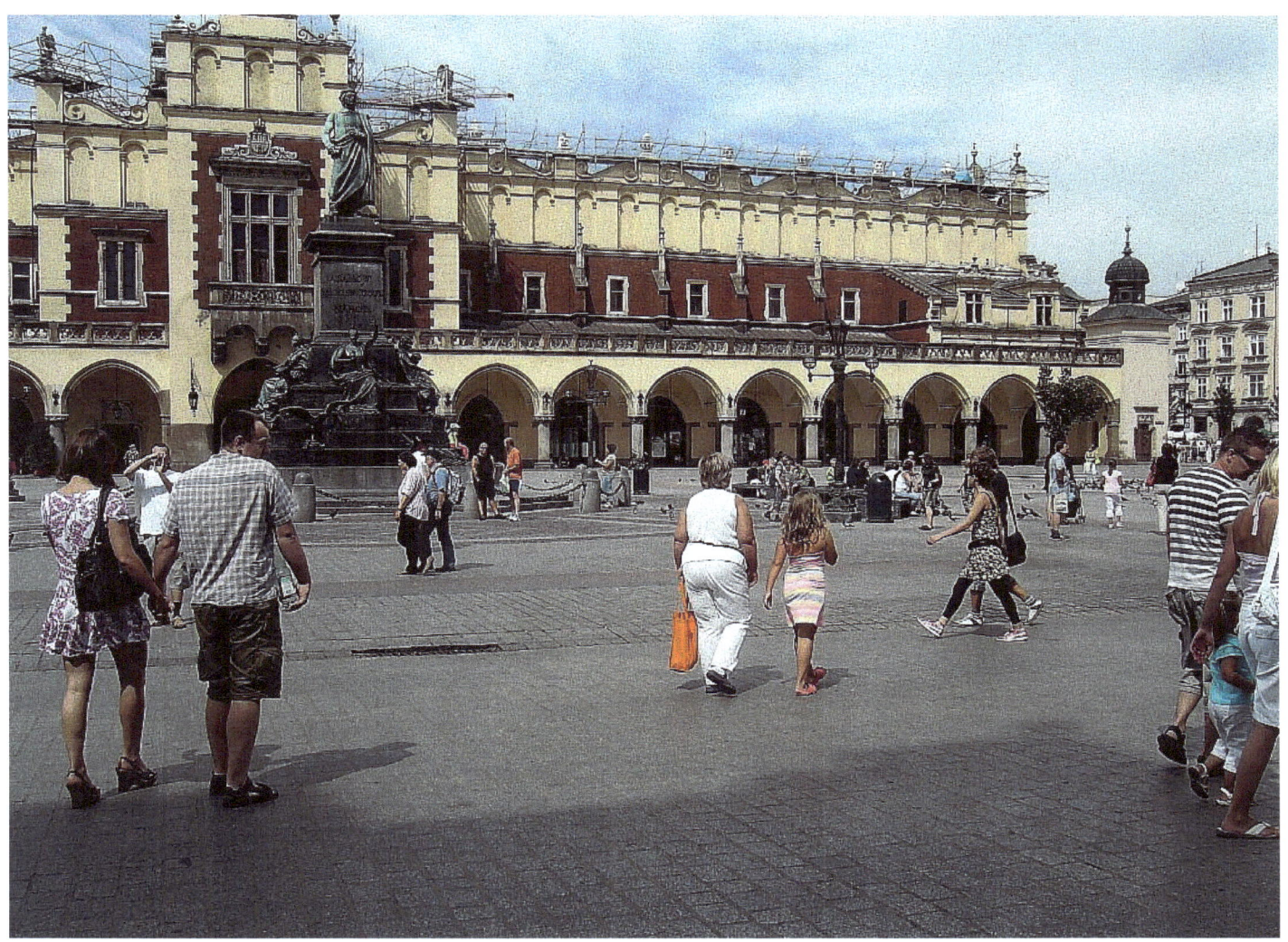

Barszcz czerwony z ziemniakami, beetroot soup and potatoes. Peel the beets and cut into cubes, put in the beef broth and cook over low heat for half an hour, along with the potatoes and a pinch of black pepper. Pass everything through a sieve and pour into the tureen, adding two teaspoons of sugar. Cook the hard-boiled eggs, cool and cut into cubes. Mix the fresh cream with the juice of four lemons in a bowl and add to the tureen, adding the hard-boiled eggs and the ice cubes. When the cubes have melted, sprinkle the soup with minced dill and bring to the table.

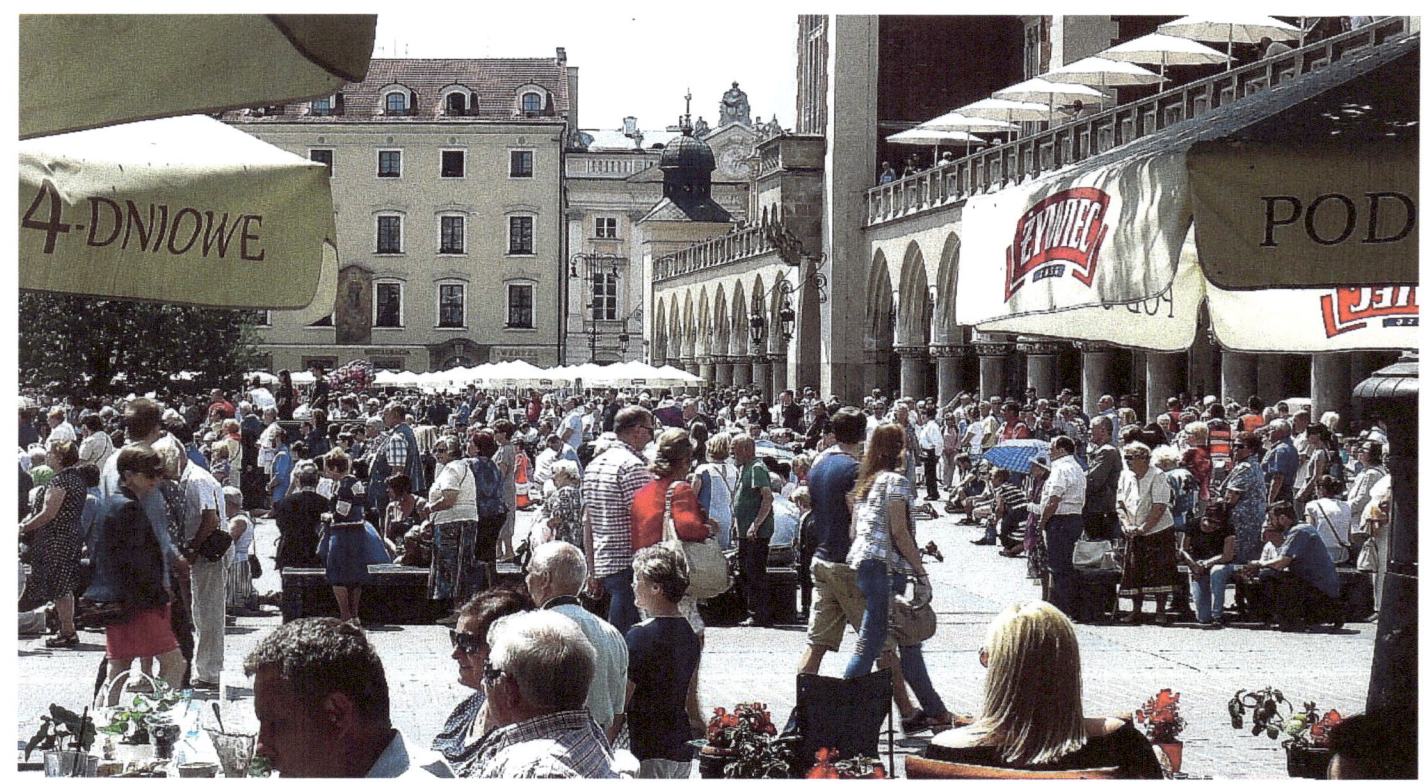

Chłodnik, cold milk soup with beet leaves, chives and cucumbers. Put the beets in salted water and bring to a boil. Lower the heat and cook for about 50 minutes. They must be hard. Drain and allow to cool. Wash the cucumbers and radishes. Peel the cucumbers and cut into cubes. Remove the leaves from the radishes, peel the garlic and put it in a blender with cucumbers and a little oil. In a bowl pour the kefir, add the fresh or dried dill and squeeze the juice of a lemon. Finally add the oil, salt and pepper. Peel the beets and cut into four, then transfer into the blender. Blend everything until obtaining a homogeneous and smooth consistency, add it to the kefir and stir. Cut the radishes into slices and add to the *chłodnik*. Serve very cold, after adding a sprinkling of dill and a drizzle of oil.

Zupa pomidorowa, tomato soup. Boil the beef with the bone and when it is almost cooked add the carrots, celery and peeled tomatoes, all cut into small pieces. When everything is cooked, add salt and pepper and add boiled rice. Serve hot.

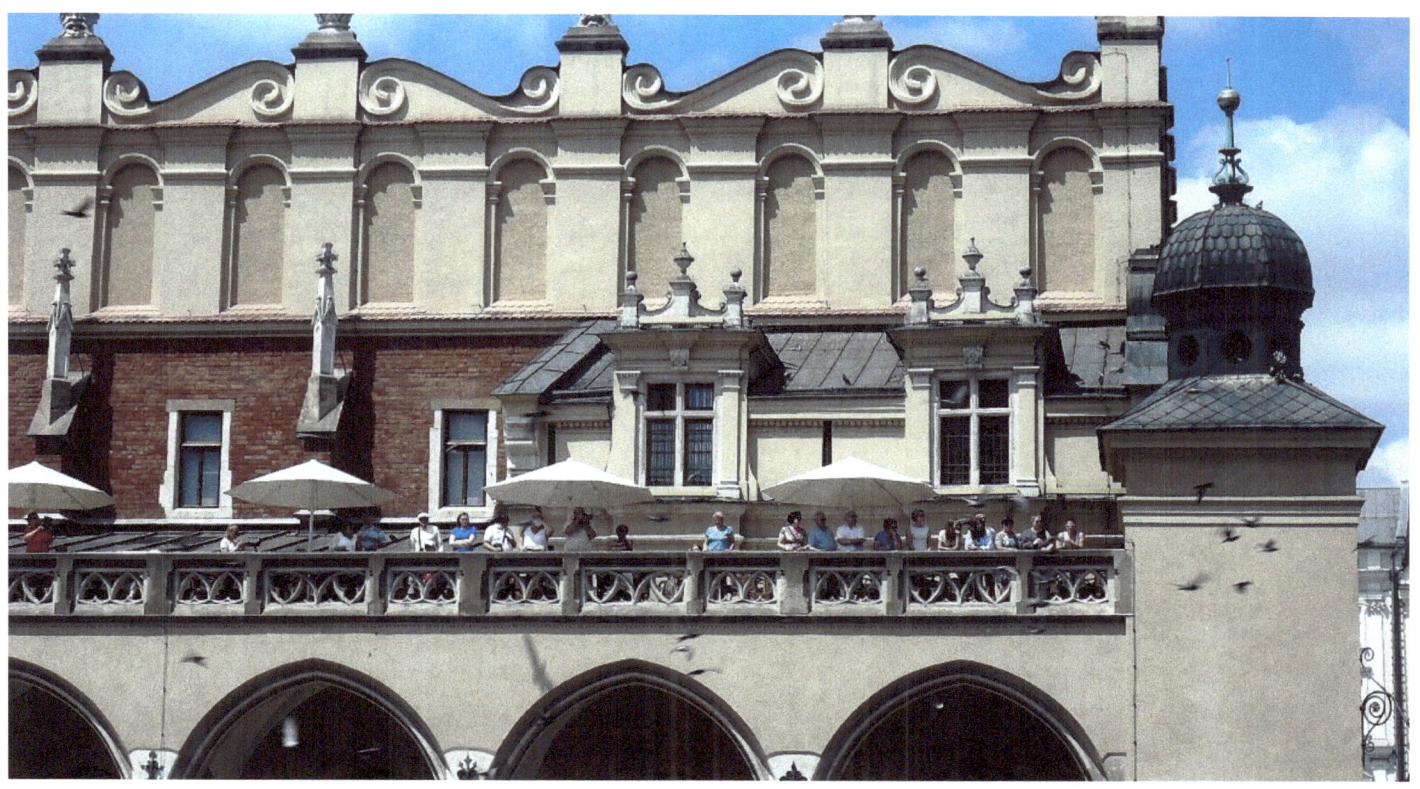

Czernina, duck blood soup. Mix the fresh blood of a freshly killed duck (or goose) with half a cup of vinegar so that it does not coagulate and store it in the refrigerator until ready for use in a covered glass container. Put the pieces of duck in a large pot and cover with at least 10 cups of cold water. Bring to a boil and remove the foam. Add a bay leaf and other spices to taste like marjoram and thyme. Salt and pepper. Cook over a low heat, partially covered for one hour. Add the dried fruit (prunes, raisins, pears, apples) and cook another hour. Remove the meat from the bones and put back in the pot. Let the soup cool in the refrigerator to more easily remove the grease and prevent coagulation once you add the blood. When the soup is cold, pour a part into a large bowl, add a few tablespoons of flour and mix well with a fork. Add 3 ladles of cold soup and the mixture of blood and vinegar and blend well. Put everything back in the pot with the remaining soup and warm over a low heat for about 30 minutes until a thicker soup is obtained. Adjust the seasonings if necessary. Serve with *kluski* or potato gnocchi.

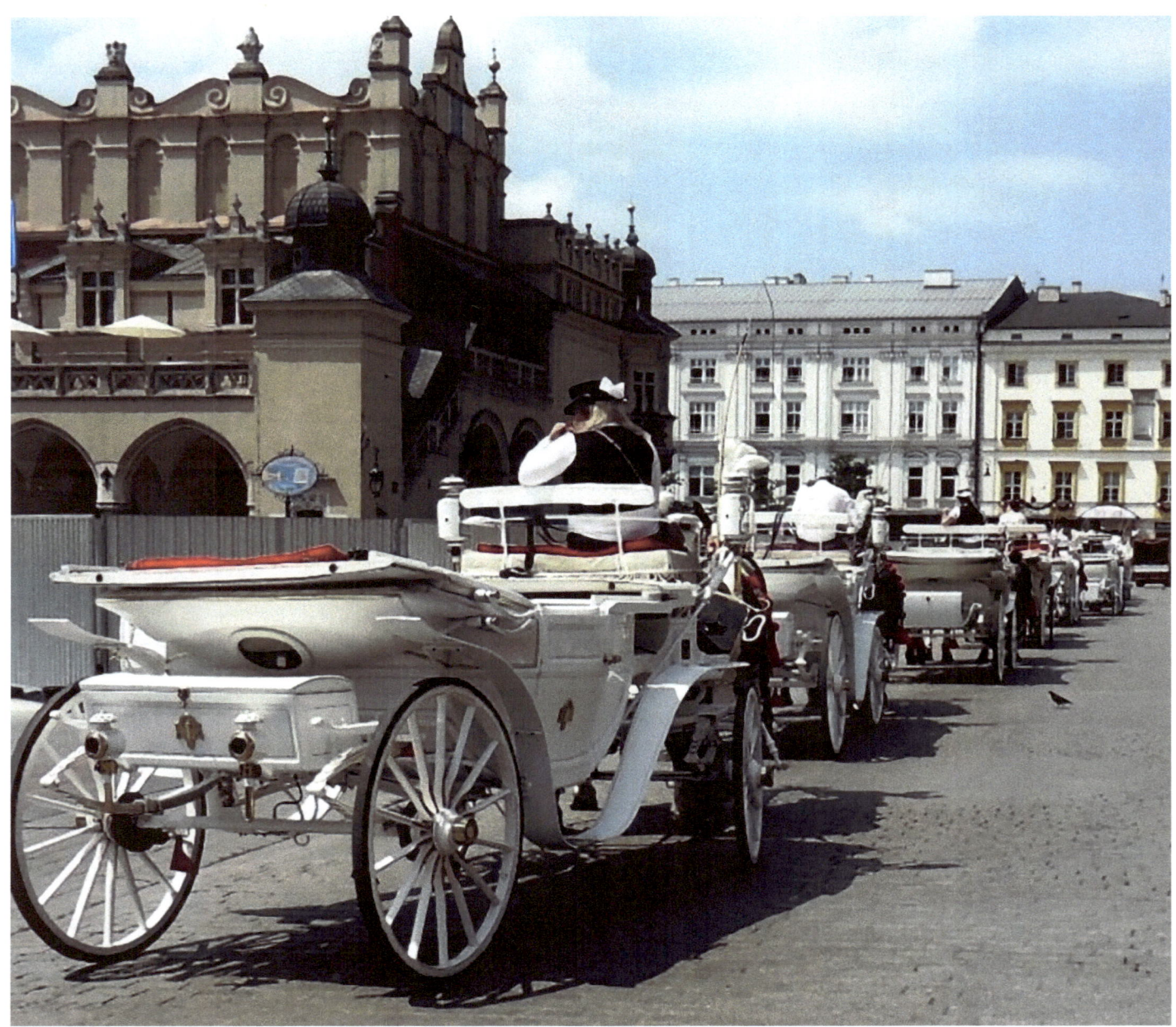

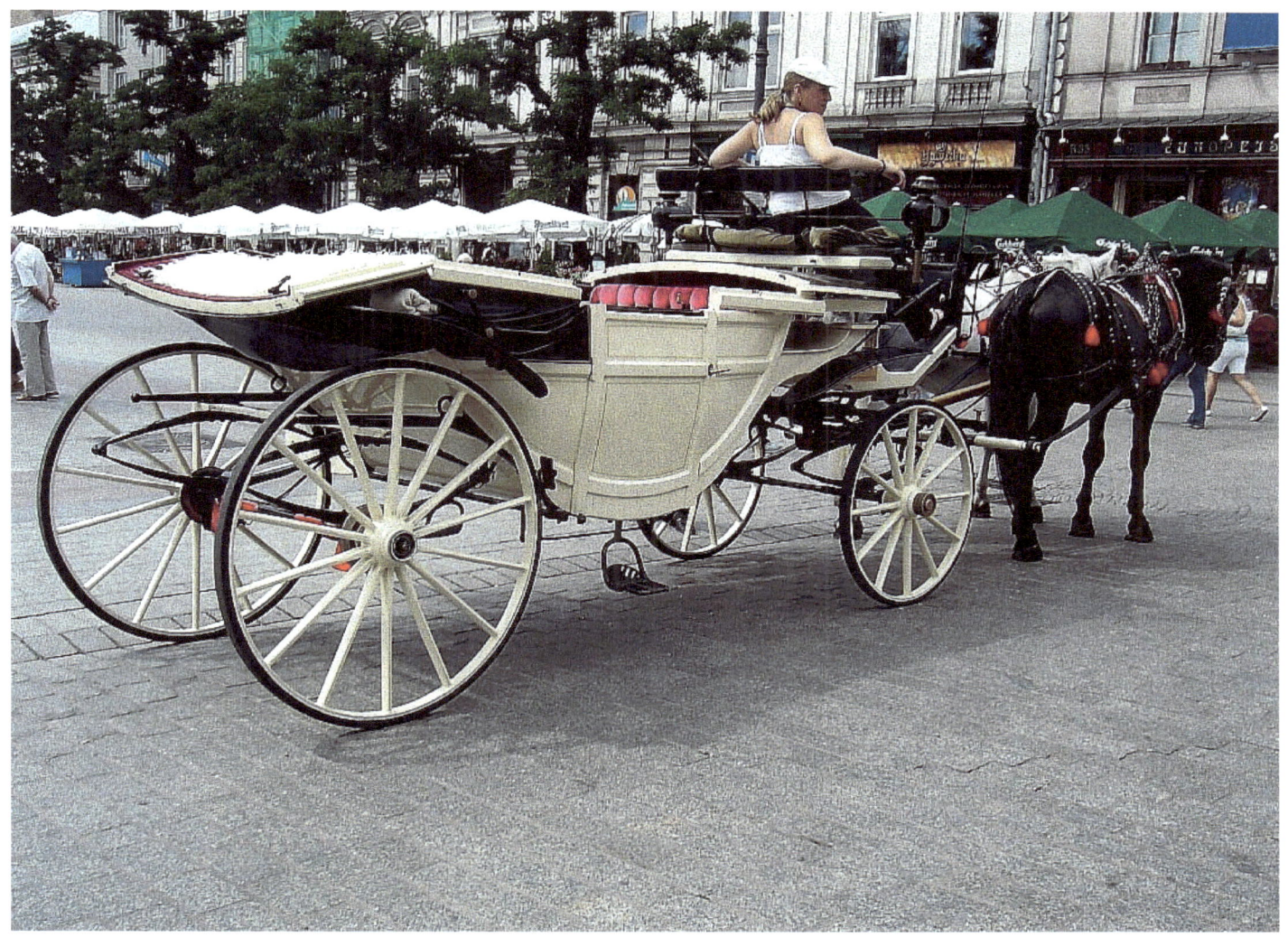

Krupnik, beef soup. Mix 200g of pearl barley with a liter of meat stock in a large saucepan. Bring to a boil, lower the heat and simmer until the stock is completely absorbed. Add the butter, stirring well. Boil the vegetables cut into small pieces (carrots, celery, potatoes) and, if you want, the giblets left in the broth until they become tender and crunchy. Add the barley, the dried parsley, add salt and pepper and cook until the barley becomes tender.

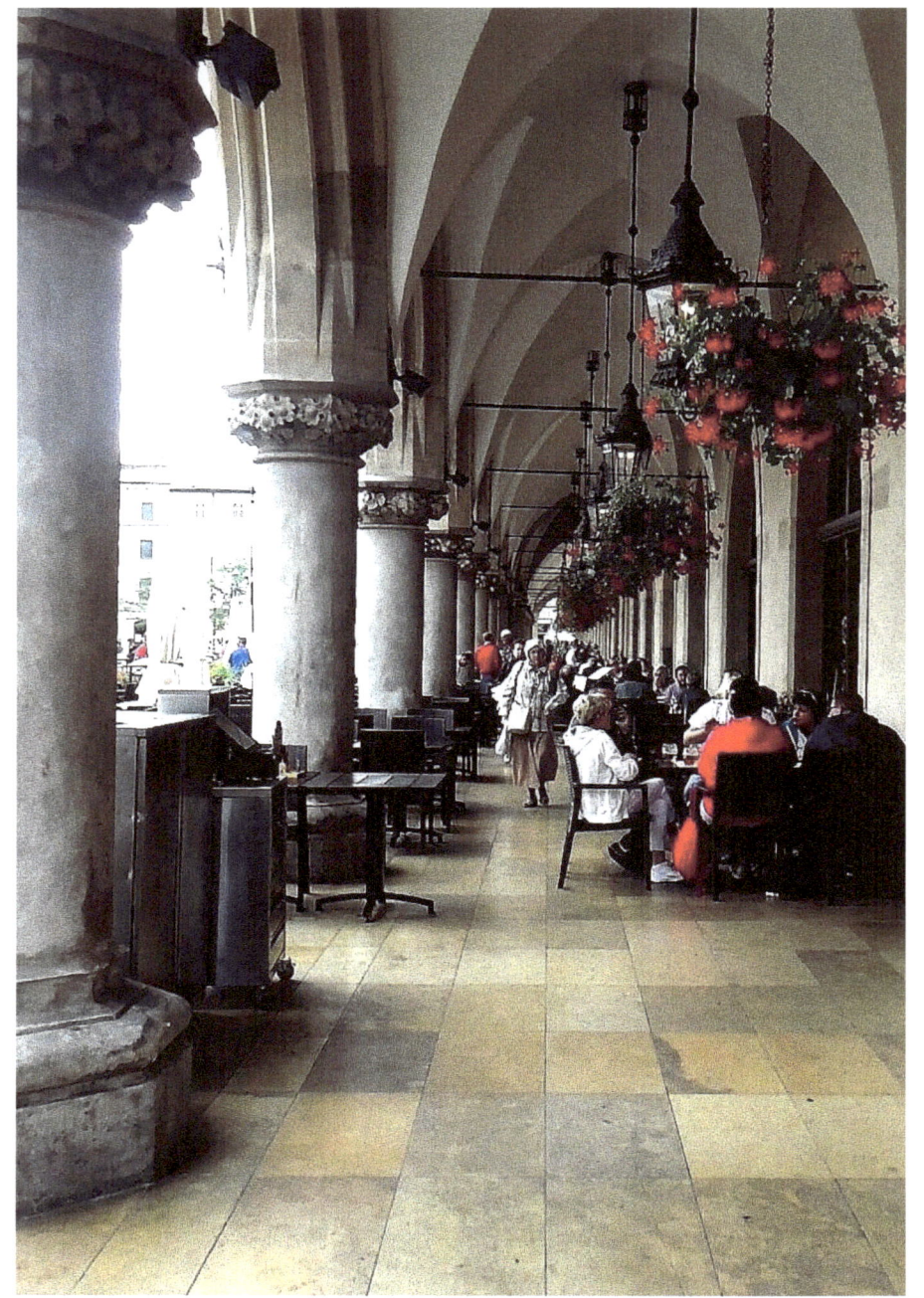

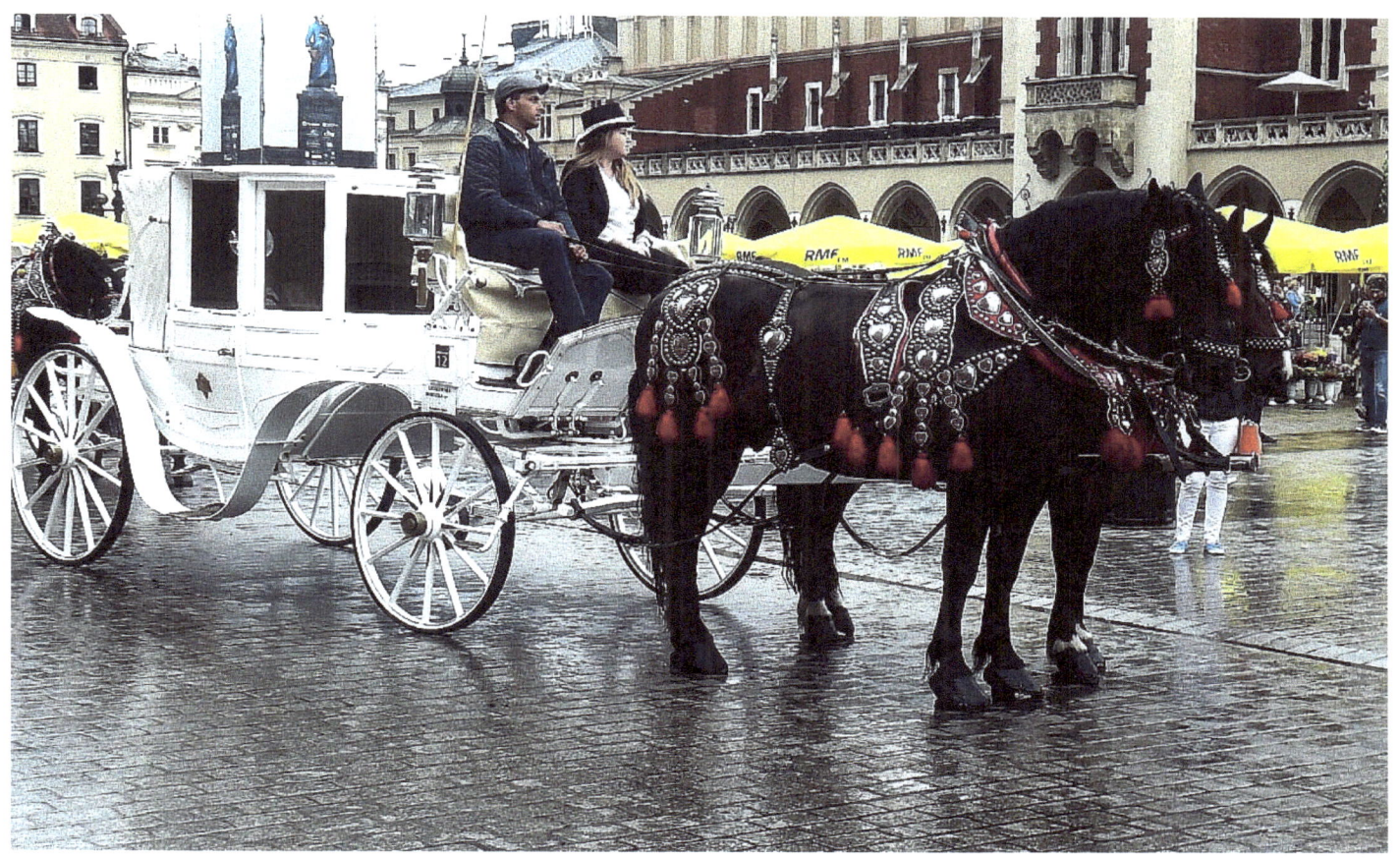

Barszcz, beetroot soup. It is a traditional Christmas Eve dish, but more generally a typical soup of the winter months. Peel the beets and cut into small pieces, then add the carrots, onions and celery into small pieces. Put everything to boil 50 minutes together with garlic, bay leaf, salt, pepper, sugar, marjoram, lemon juice, vinegar and other ingredients of your choice. *Barszcz* can be served with *uszka* (very similar to tortellini) or *pierogi*.

Flaczki, soup with pork or chicken tripe. Clean the pork or chicken tripe by scraping it with a knife and salt, washing several times under running water. Put in a pan with boiling water and cook for 15 minutes, then drain. Put back in the pot and add two liters of broth, cooking all at low heat for about 4 hours. If the cooking liquid should run out, add water. When the tripe are now boiled, take out of the pot, cut into slices and put back in the pot with the cooking base...

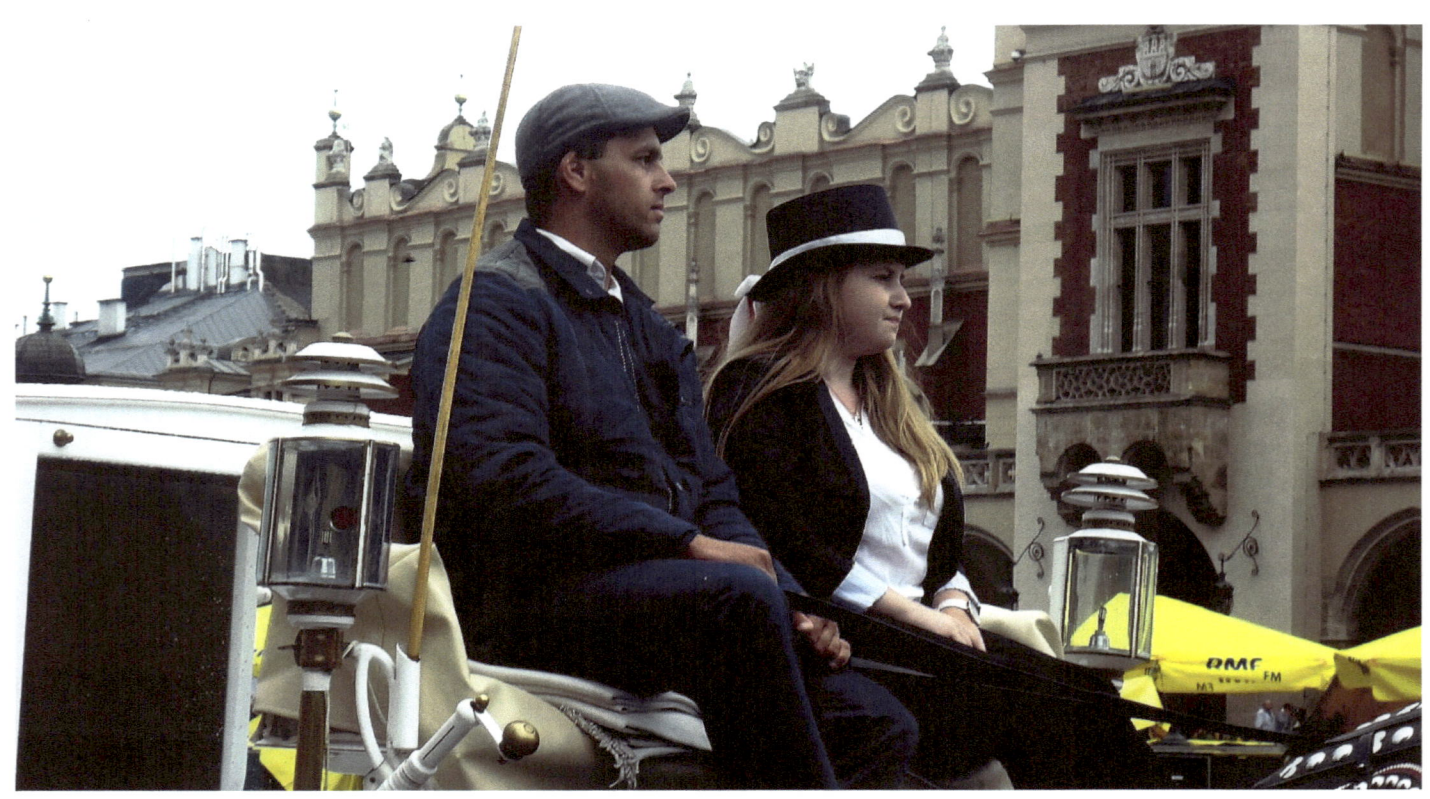

…Separately cook in a little water with a large portion of butter the vegetables (carrots, celery and leeks) previously cut. When the water is completely evaporated and the vegetables cooked add them to the tripe. Separately fry a chopped onion in the butter and when it has browned add a little flour without making lumps. Pour into the tripe and season with ginger, nutmeg, pepper and salt. Continue cooking for another 10-15 minutes.

Grochòwka, dried pea soup. Soak the dried peas for a few hours, then put them on the fire with the same water. In another pan boil the bacon with the vegetables (celery, carrots, parsley) cut into cubes. When the peas are cooked, drain and crush with a spoon until it almost forms a cream, adding, occasionally, a little water. In a pan, melt some lard, pour a tablespoon of flour and let it color. Fry the finely chopped onion aside until it browns. Remove it from the heat and mix with the flour and the mush of peas. Add a little water and mix very well until it becomes creamy. Add the vegetables, add the crushed garlic and a little salty and put on the fire for a few minutes together with the marjoram and the bacon to flavor. Serve hot.

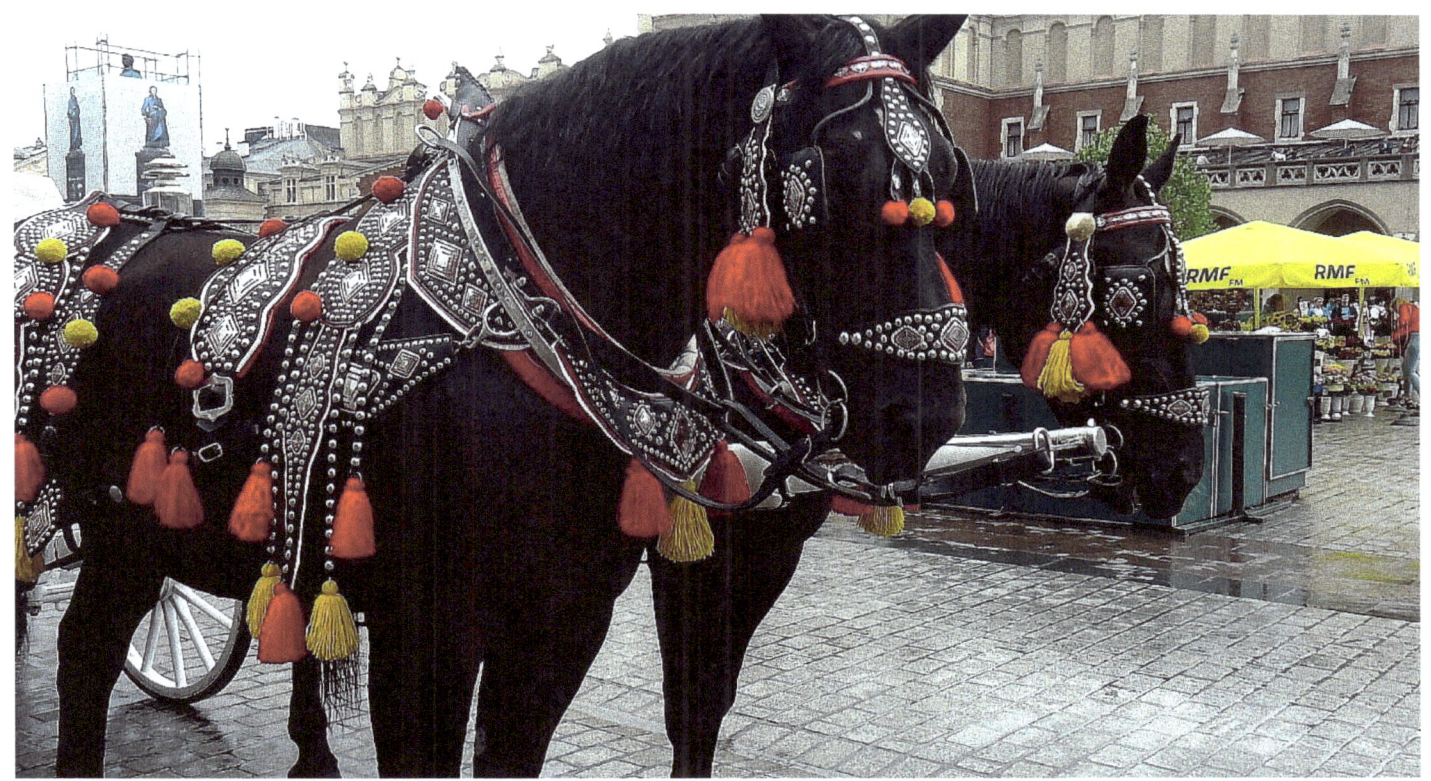

Kapuśniak, cabbage and shin soup. Take a pork knuckle and cook in a pot with 2 liters of water for about 20 minutes. Fry and add the sliced onions, a bay leaf, chopped parsley and a sprinkling of pepper. Cook for 45 minutes until the meat becomes tender. When it is ready remove from the broth, remove the bone, cut it into pieces and put back in the pot. Rinse the sauerkraut in cold water and drain, add the shin meat, plenty of raisins and let them simmer for an hour. Mix a little 'flour with the same margarine until you get a homogeneous mixture. Add to the meat soup and cook over medium heat until it thickens. Season with salt and pepper before serving.

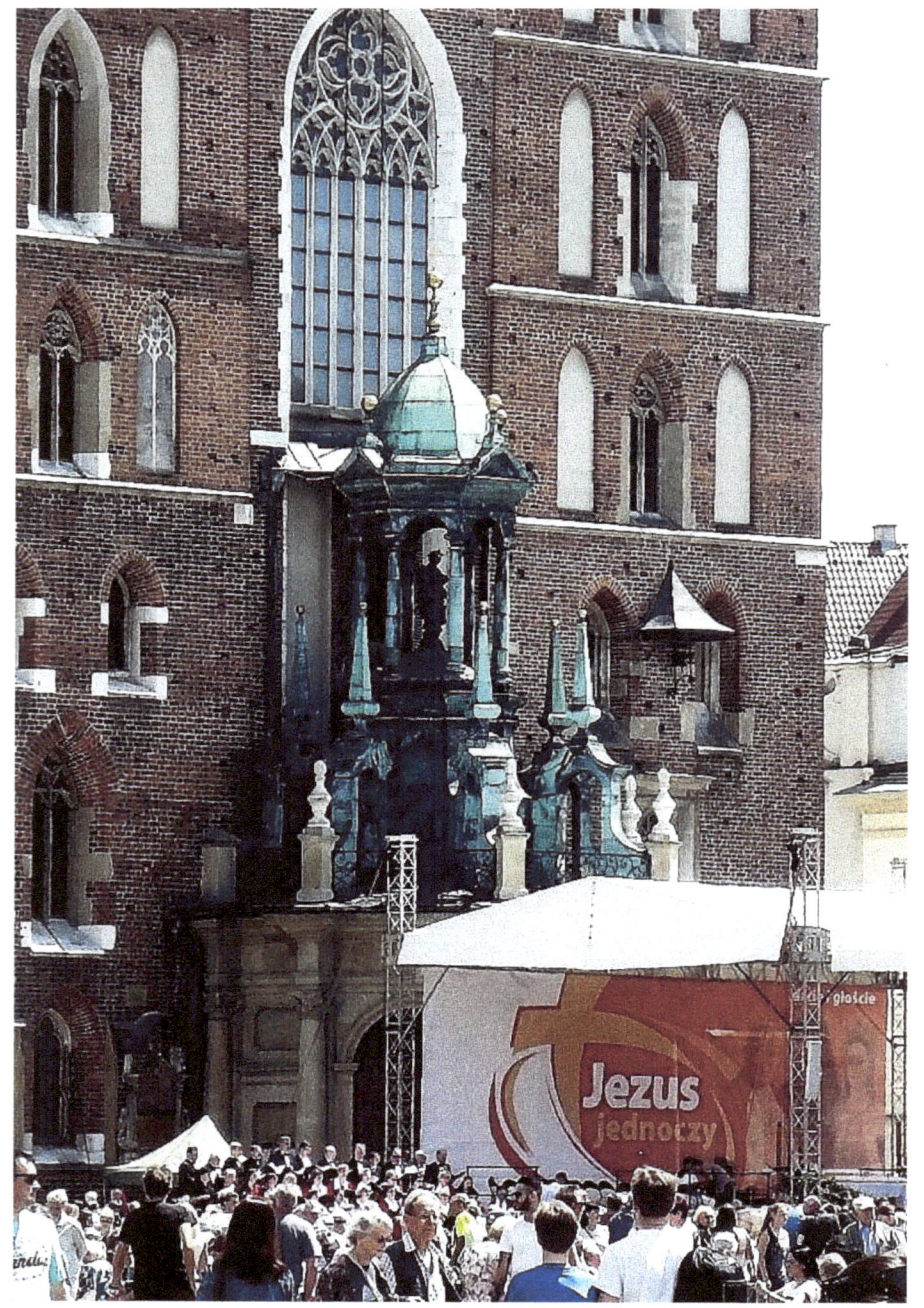

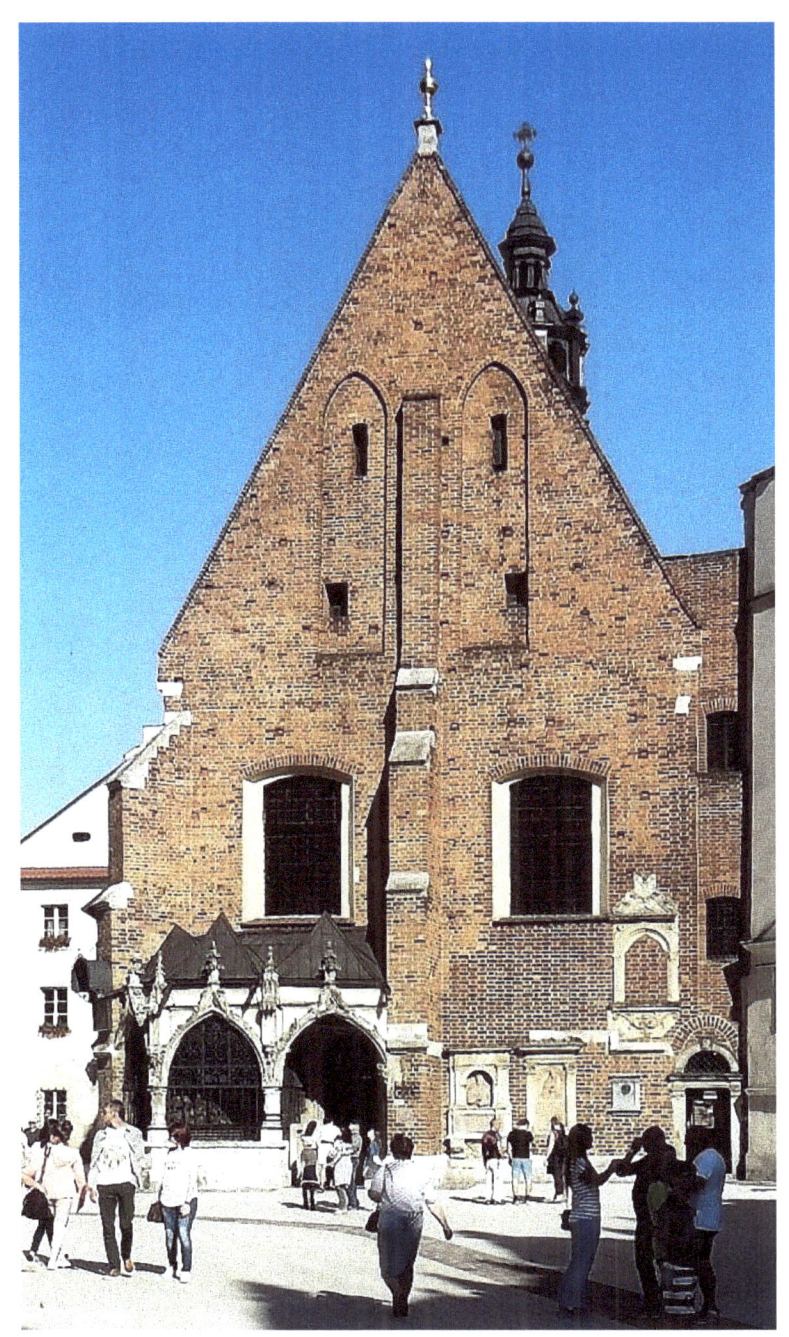

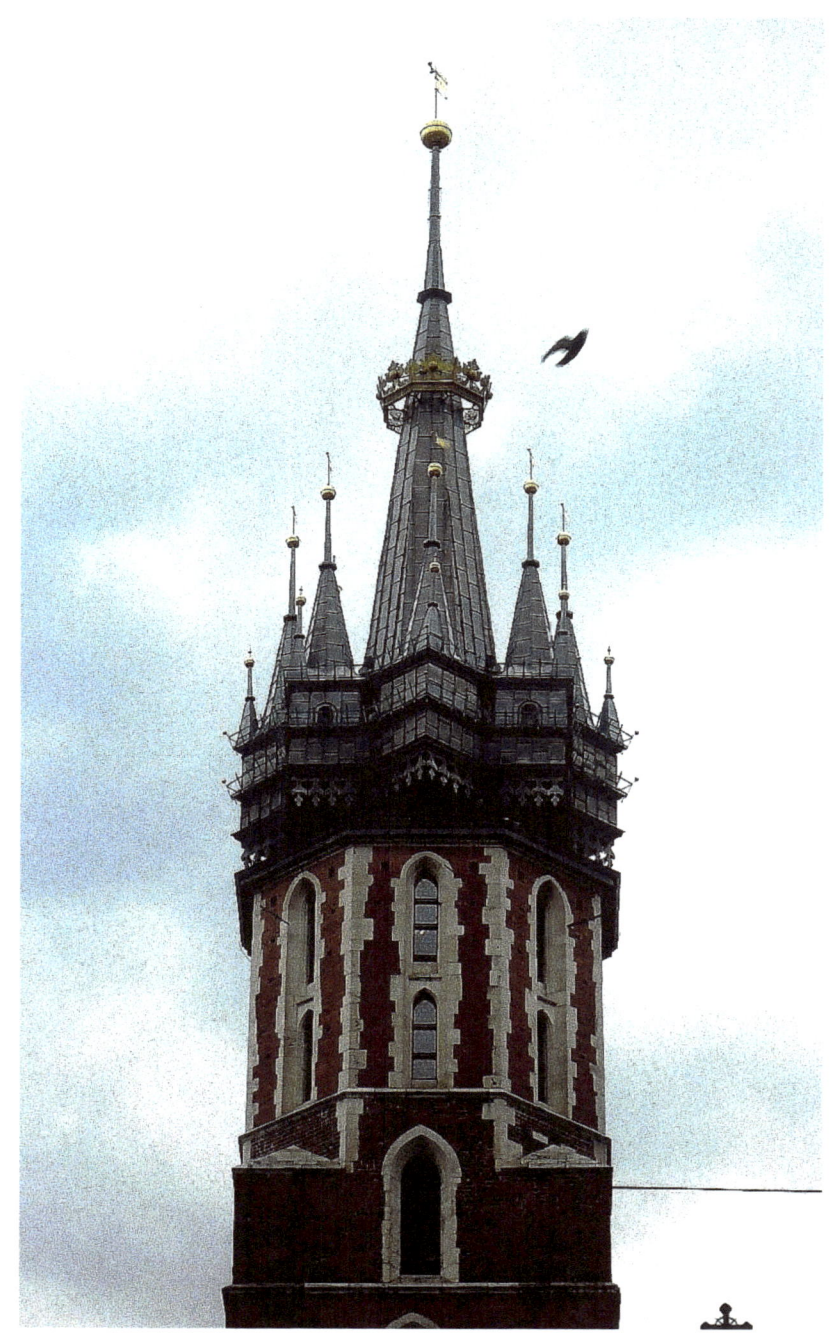

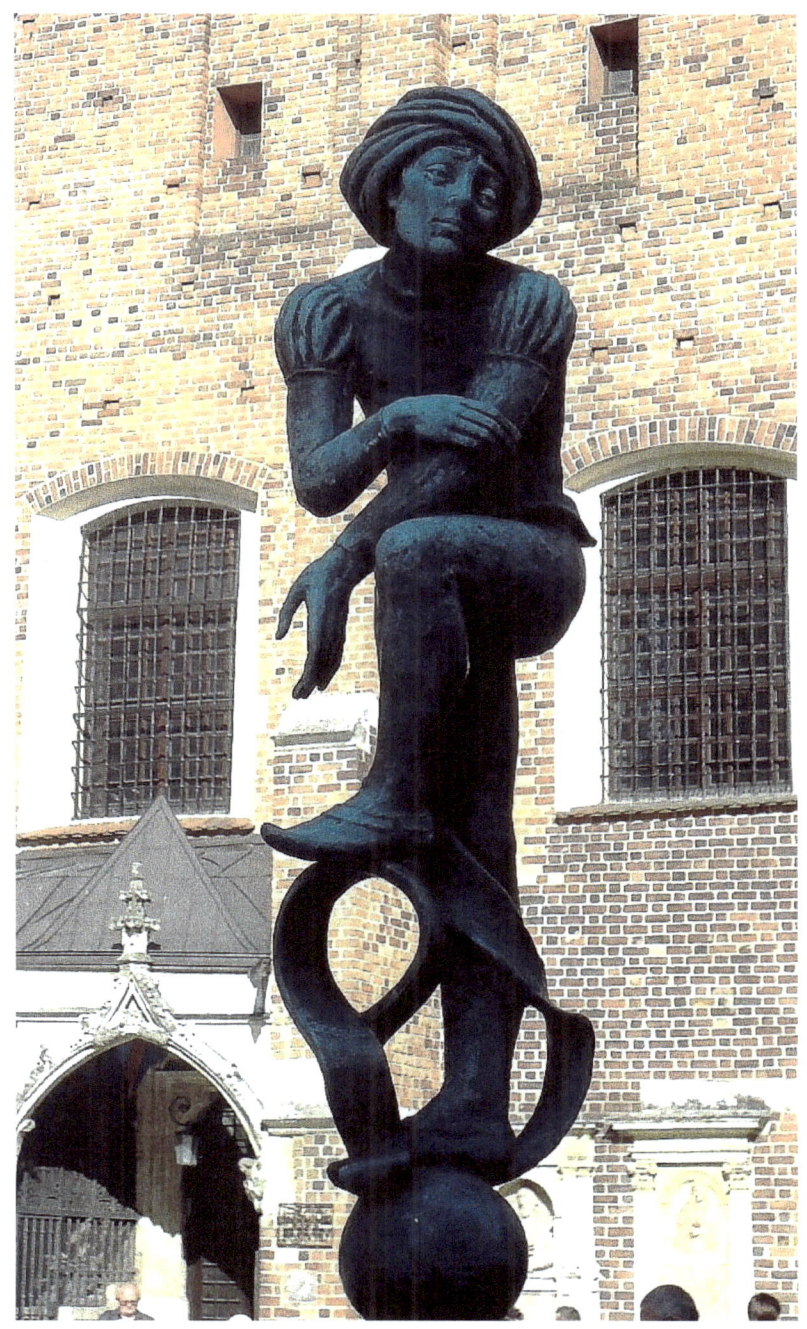

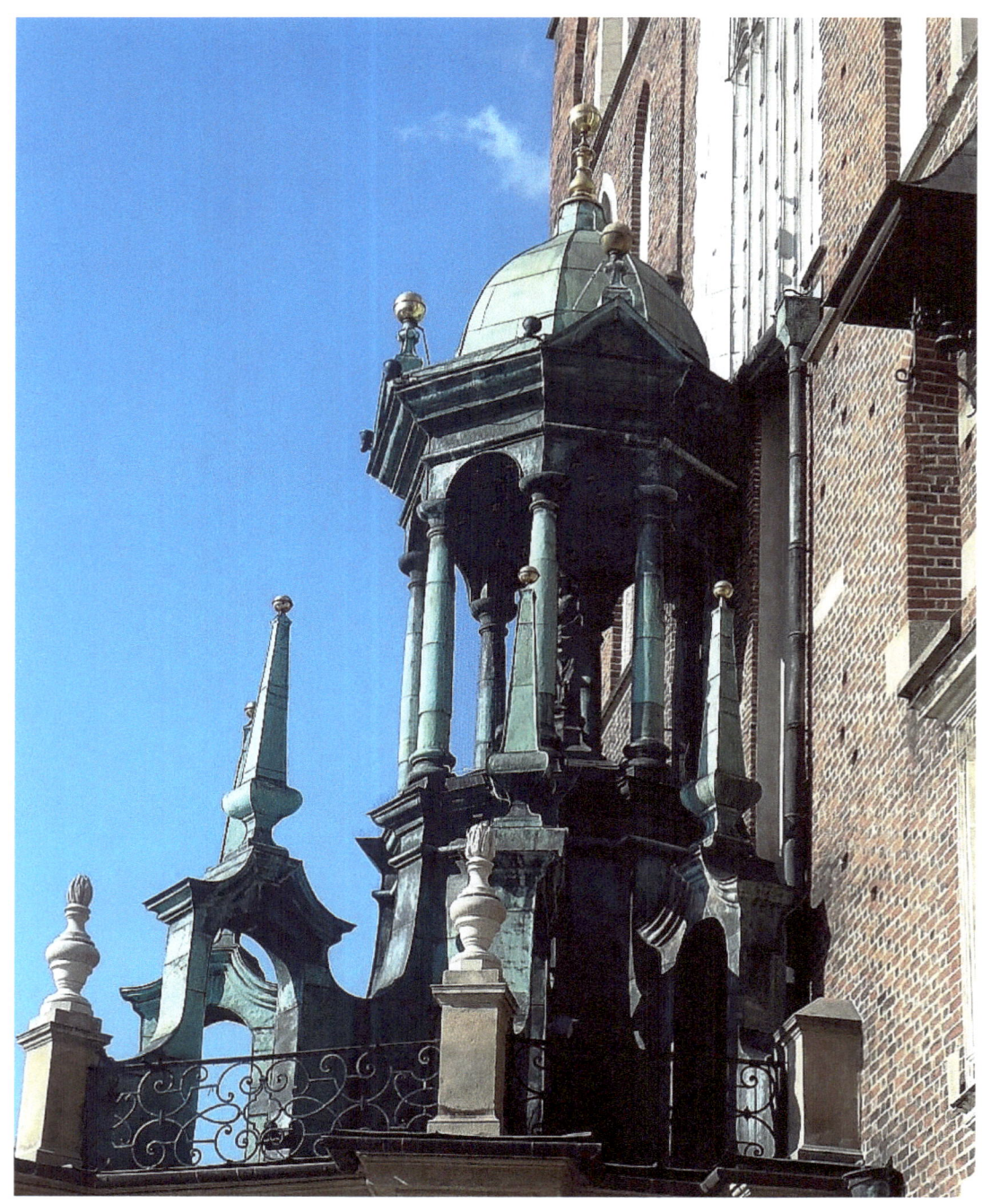

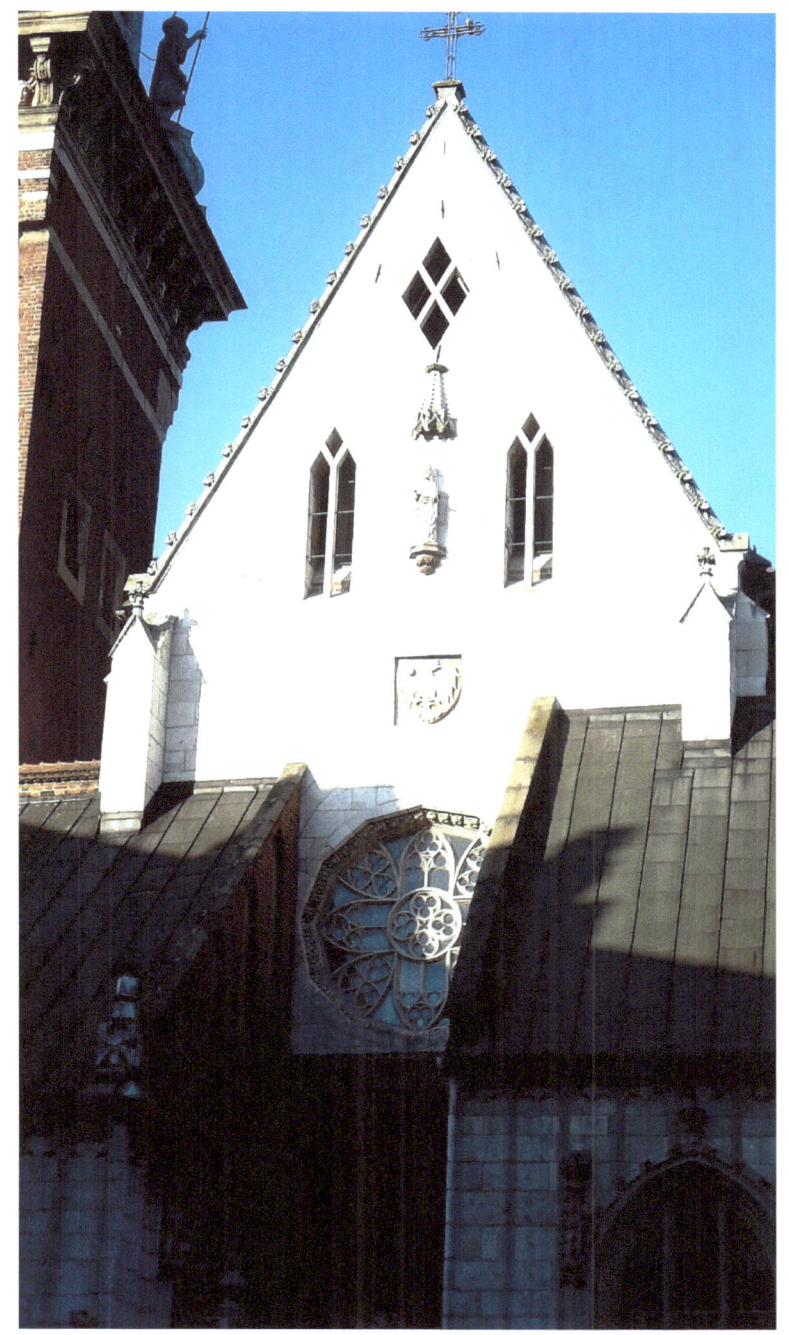

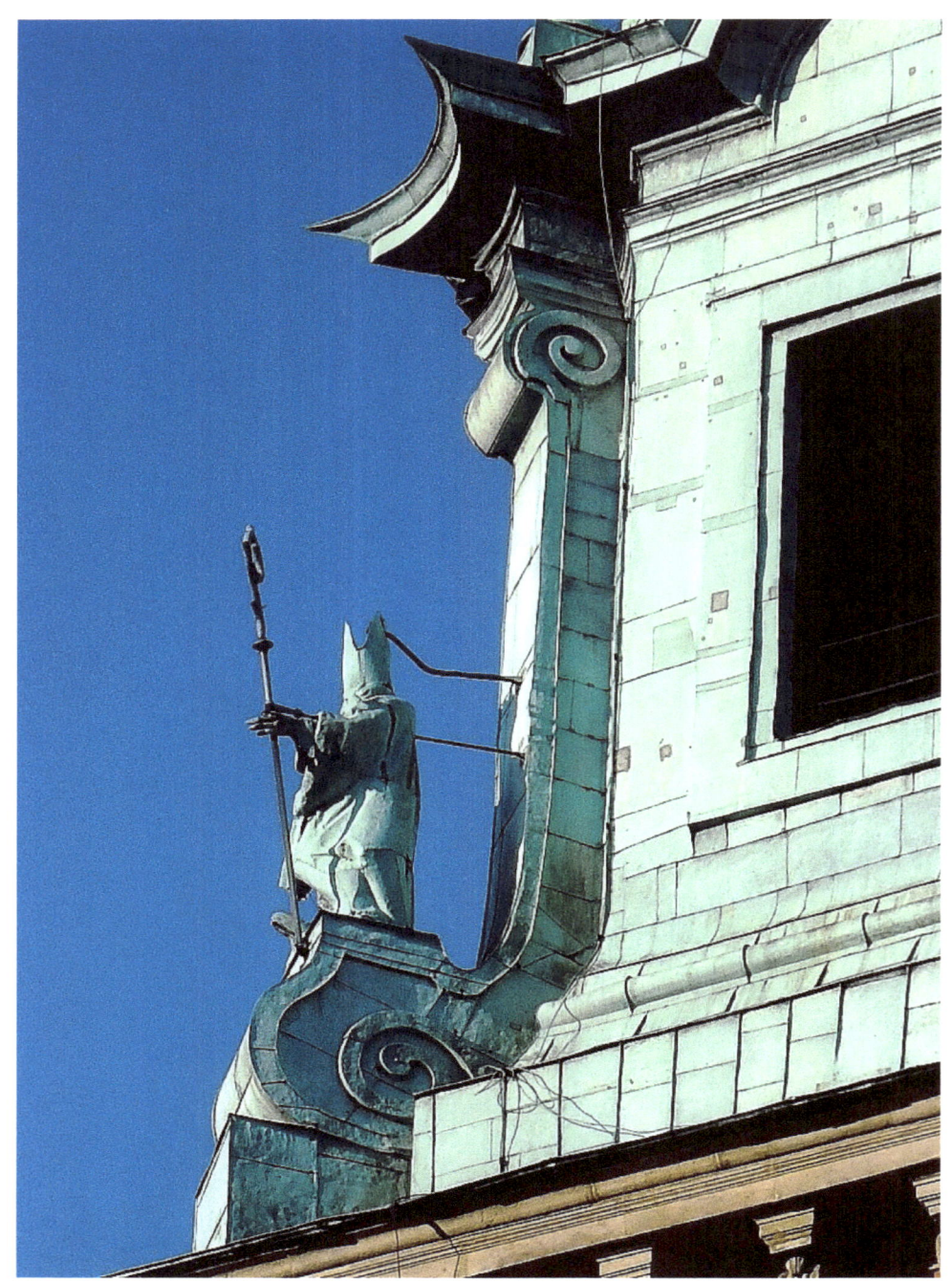

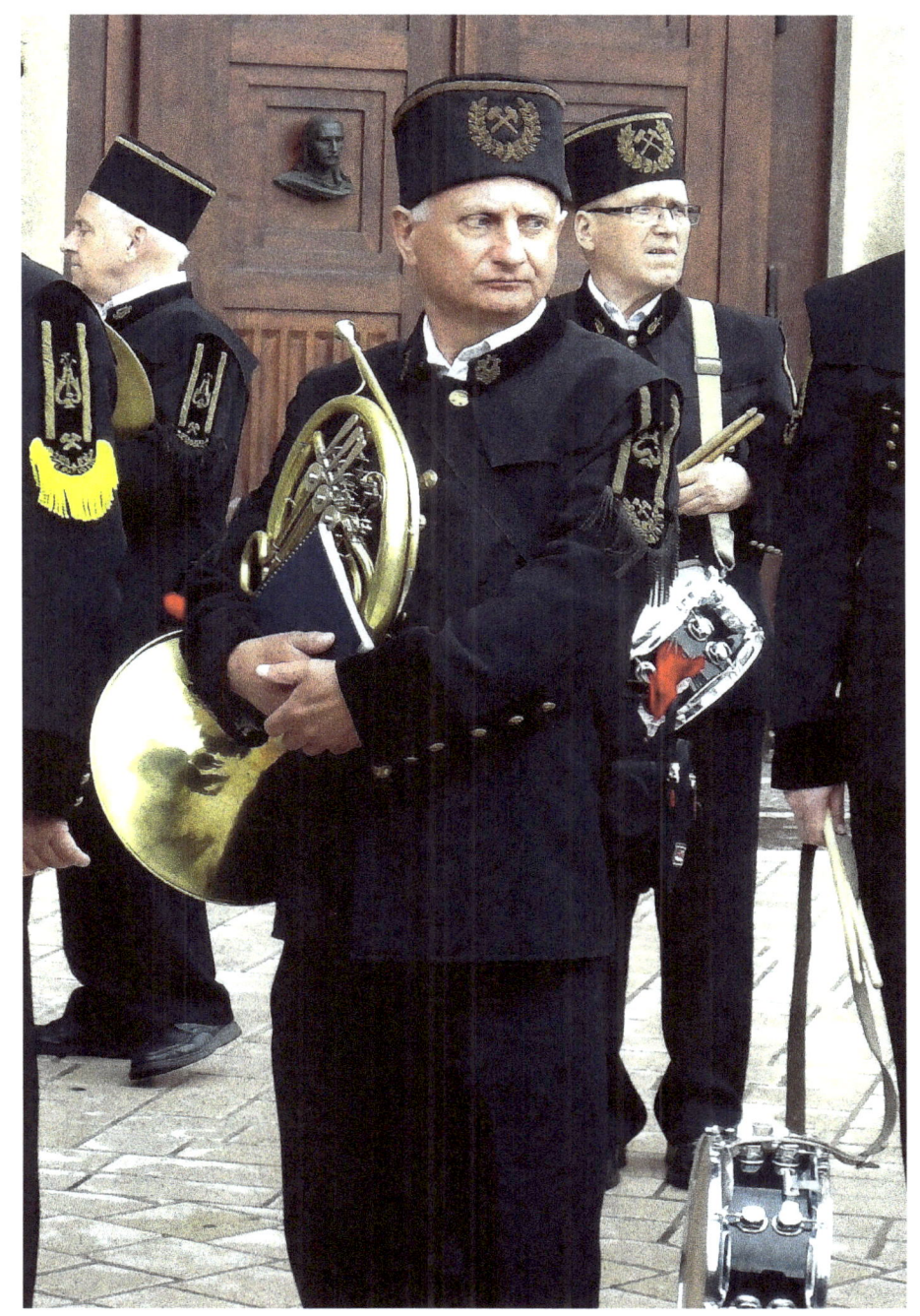

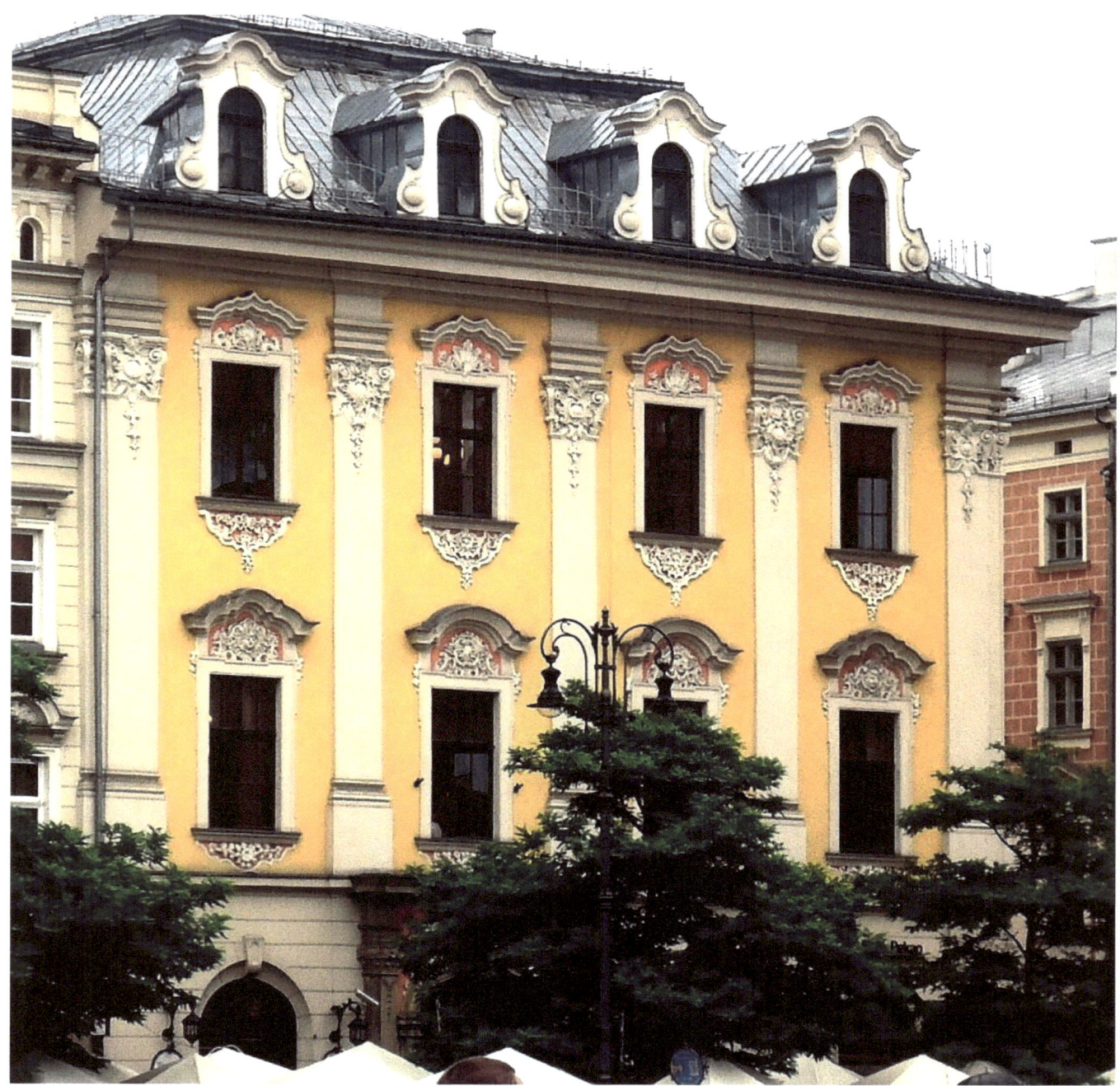

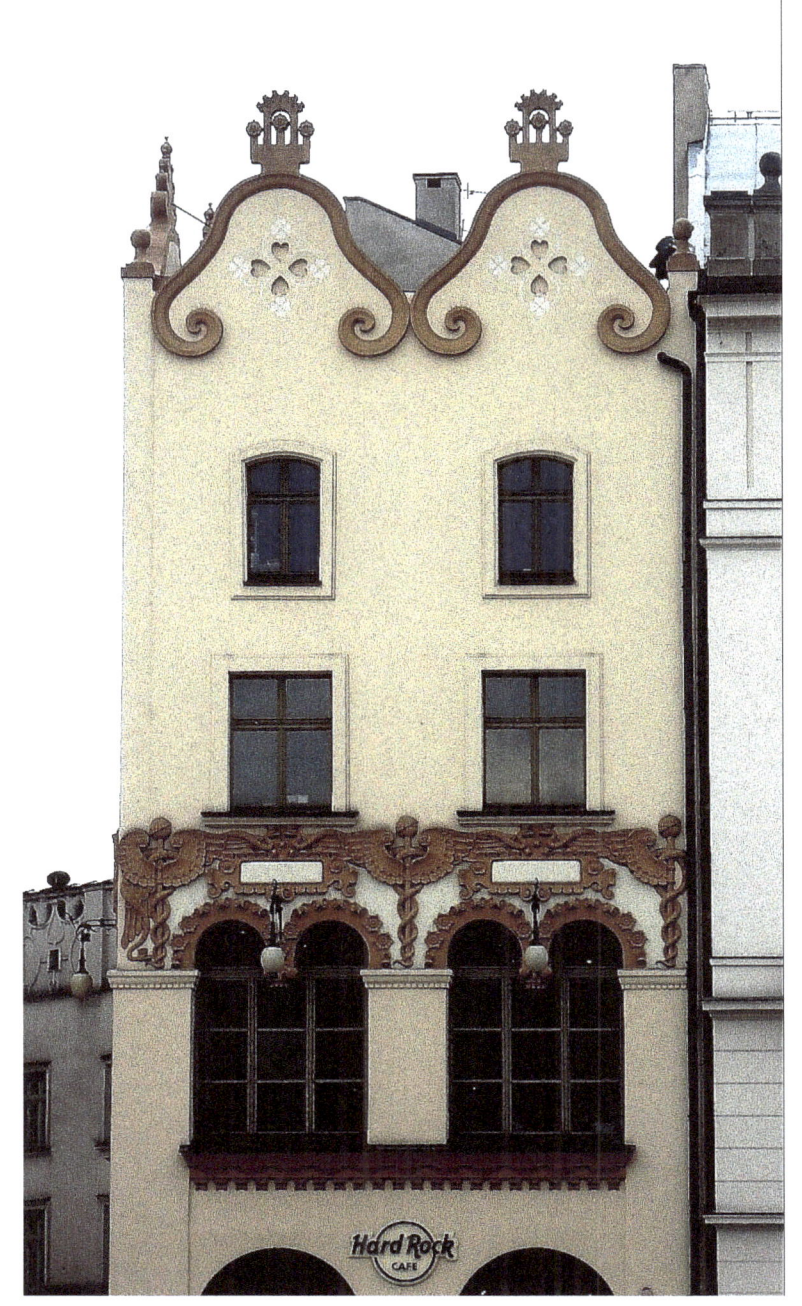

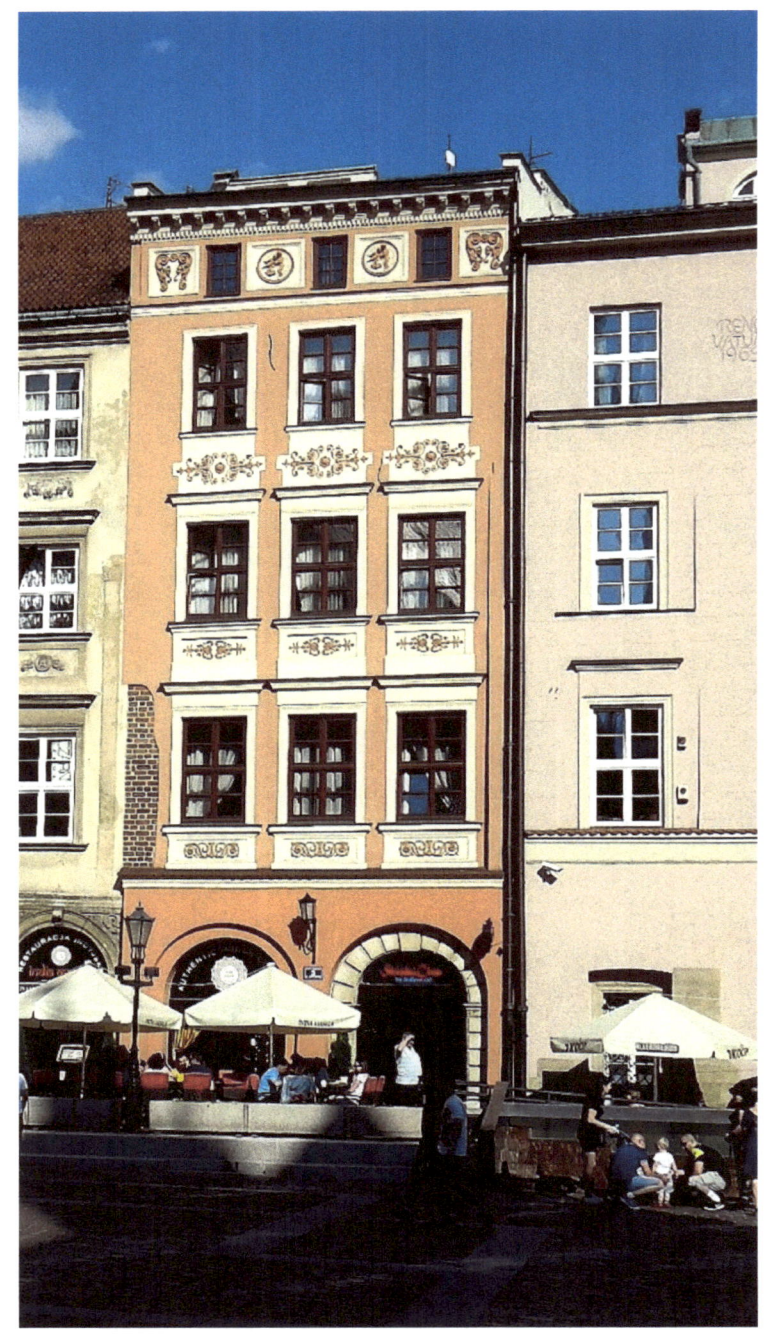

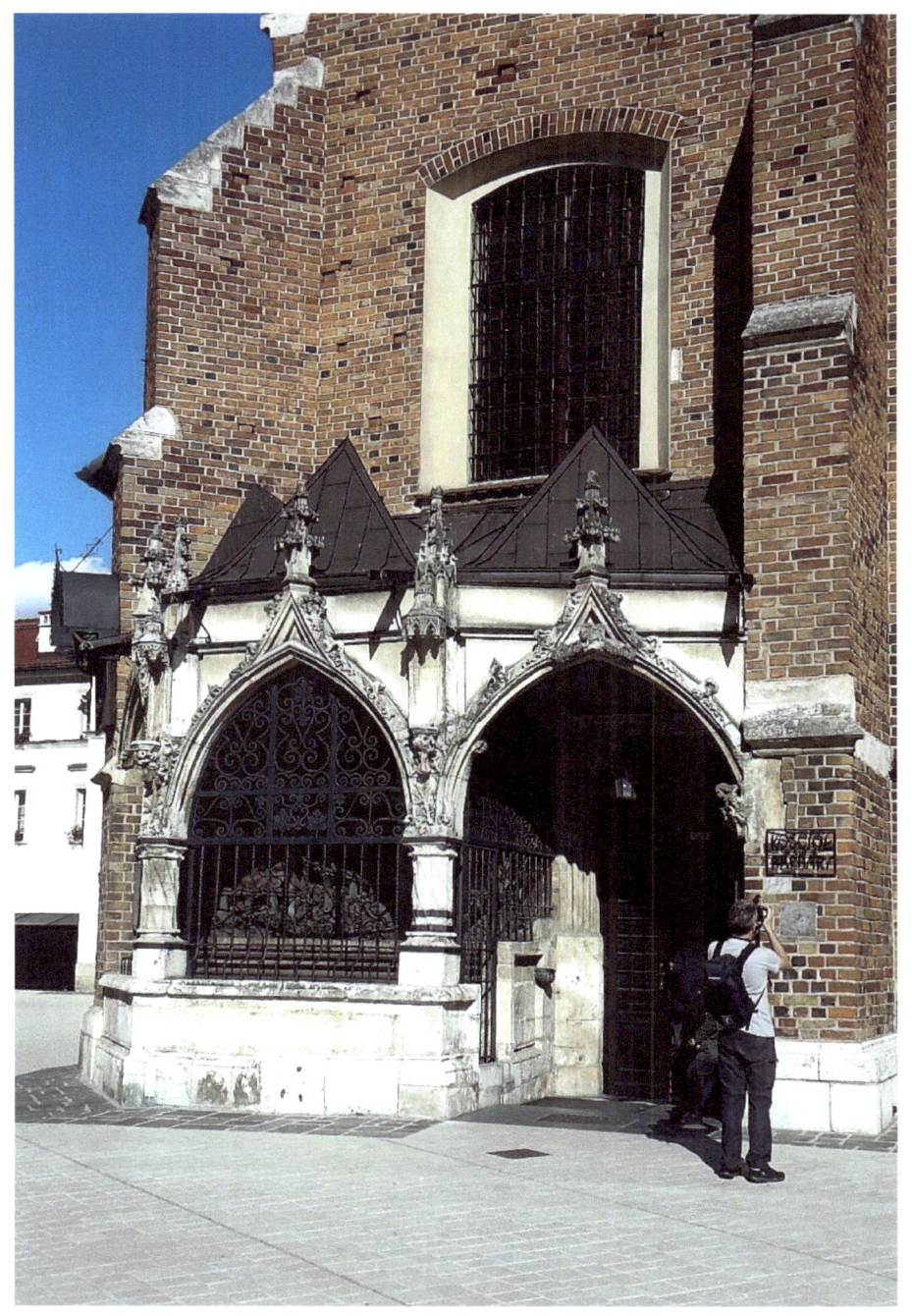

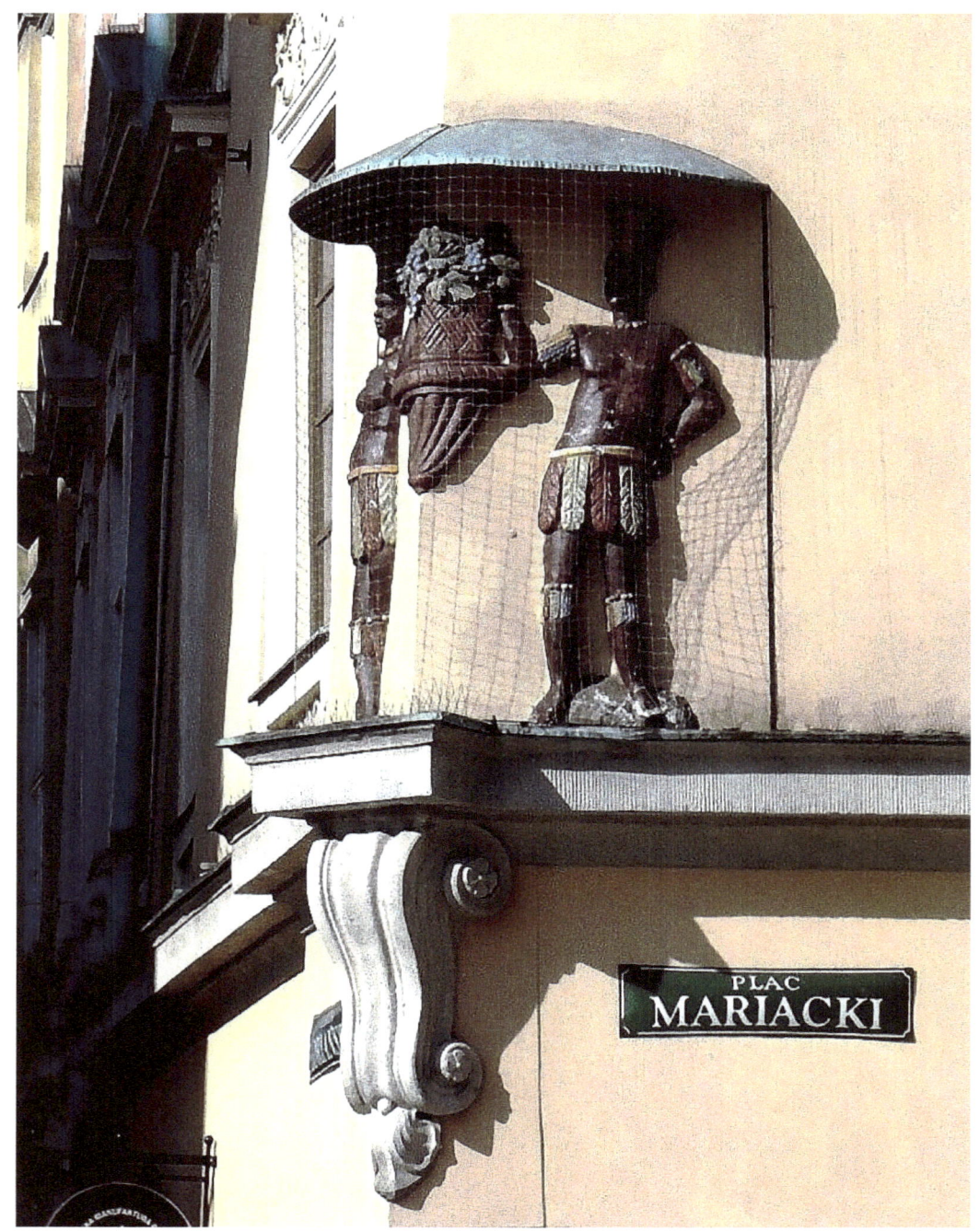

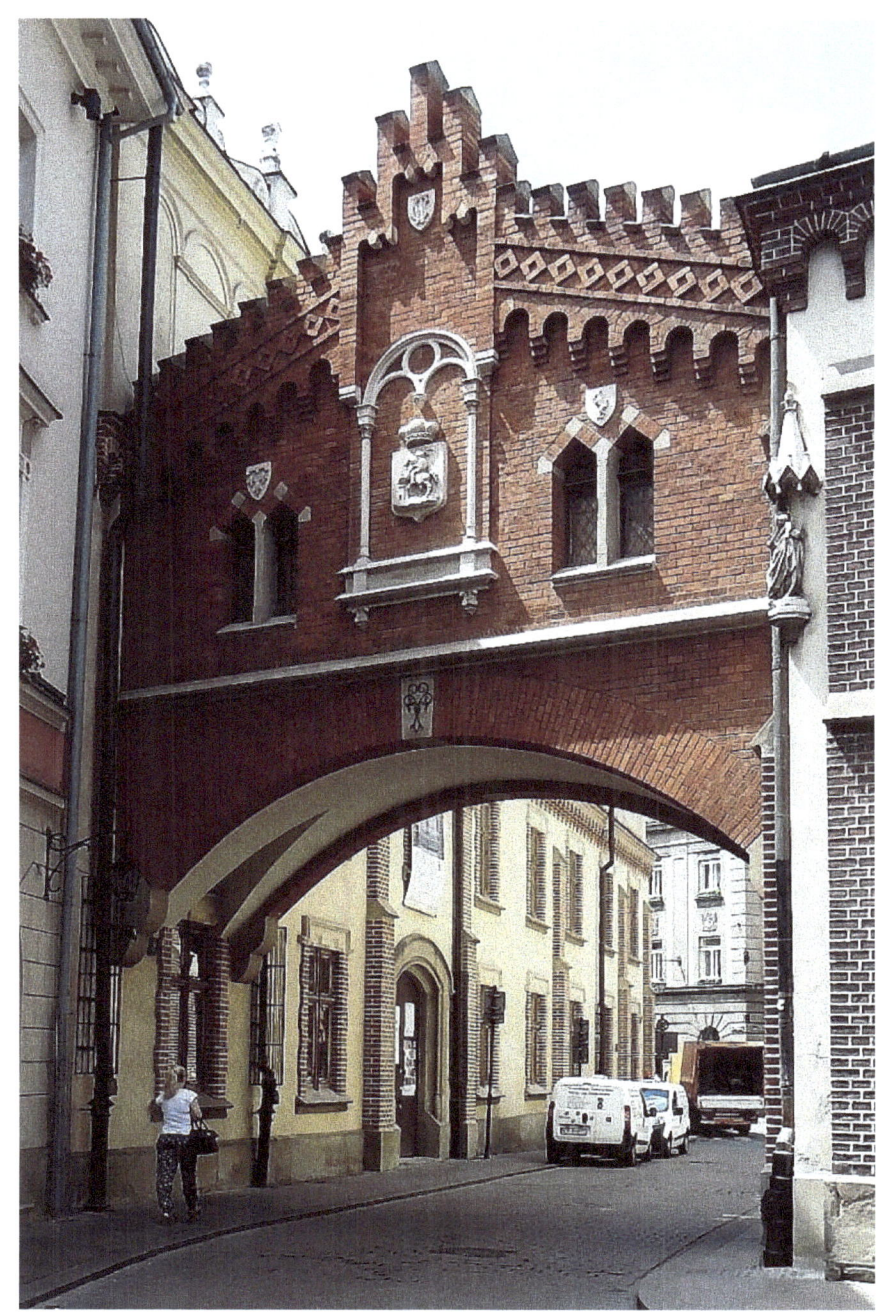

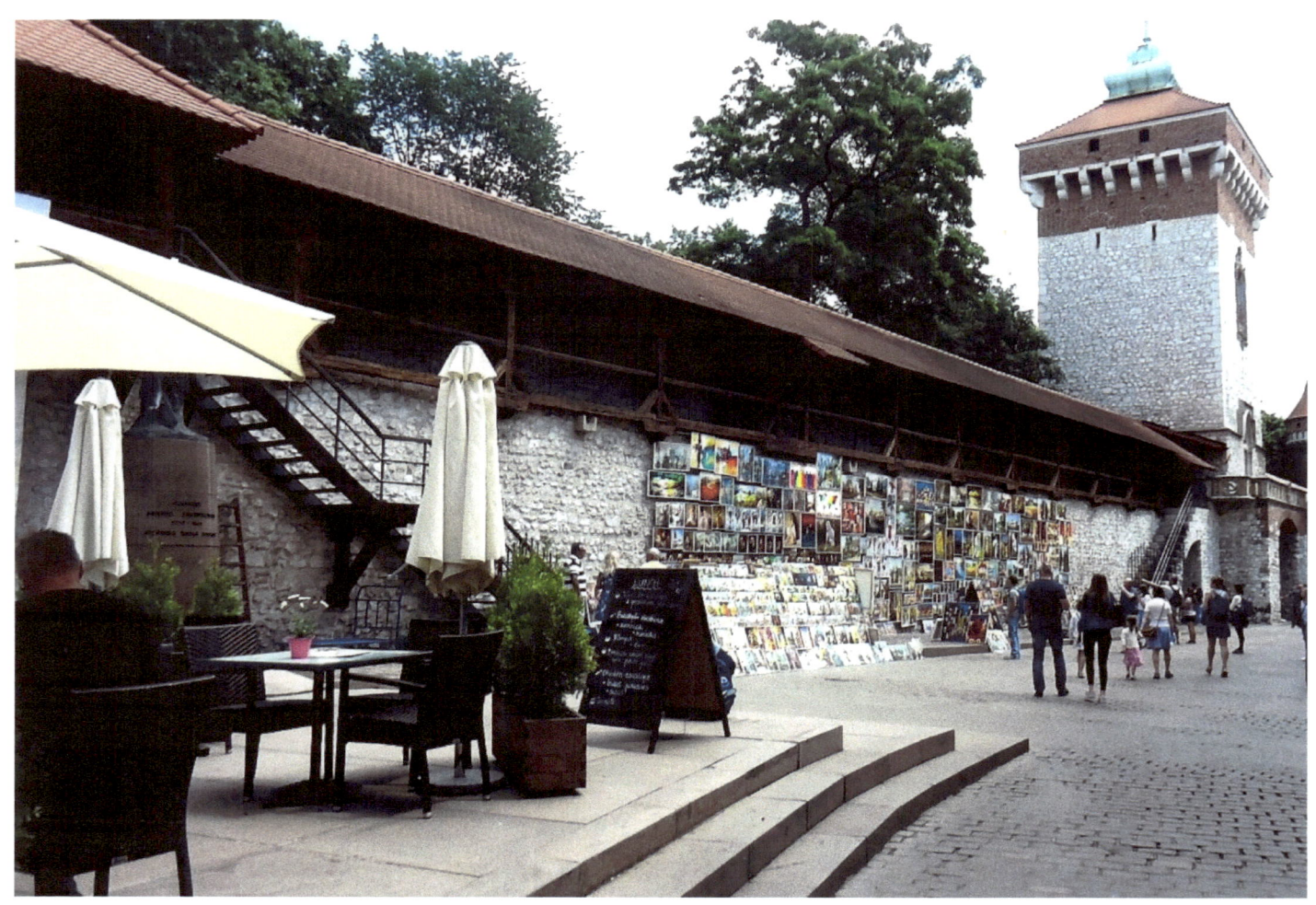

Żurek, it is the traditional Easter soup with sour rye flour, sausages and potatoes, sometimes with hard-boiled eggs cut in half. Preparation of the *żurek* acid base (*zakwas*): pour the rye flour into a glass tray, add the slightly crushed garlic, a little water, allspice, bay leaf, pepper and a few crust of wholemeal bread, cover with water and mix well. Close the tray with a lid to let the air pass, cover with a napkin and leave to stand for 3 days at room temperature. After 3 days, skim and mix the liquid, filter it and transfer to a bottle, close it well and place in the fridge. Here you can keep it for at least 10 days…

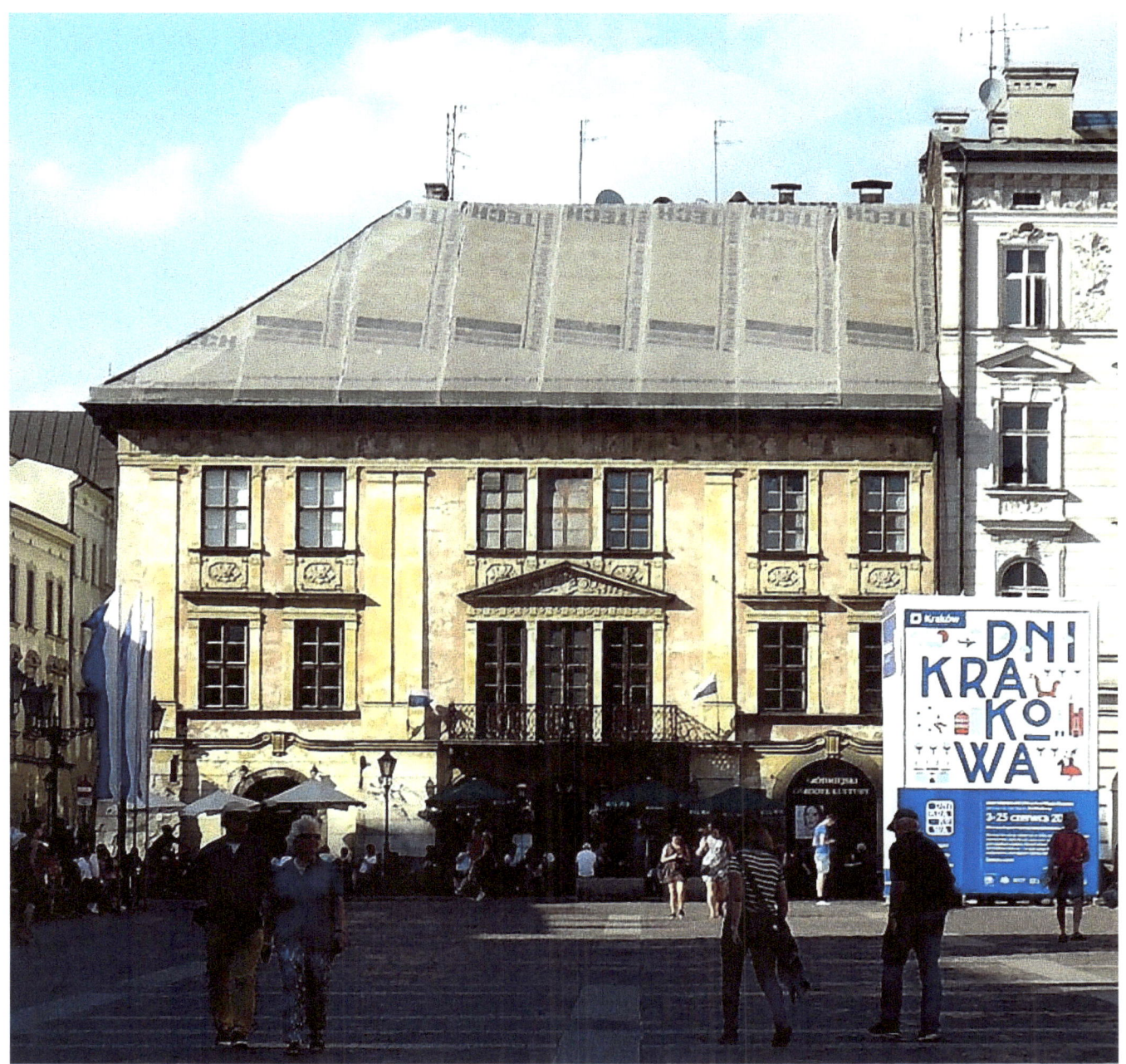

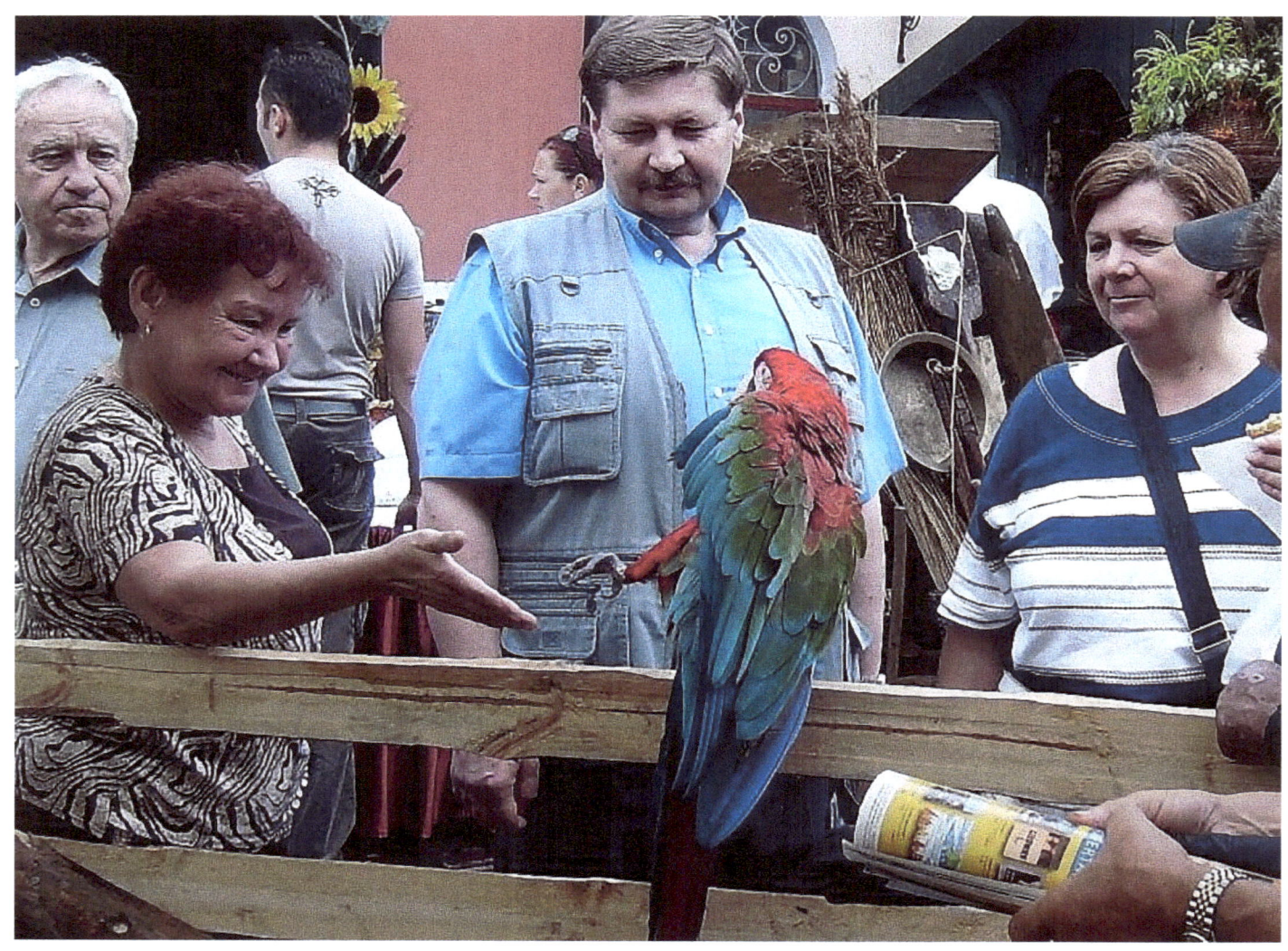

…Let the dried mushrooms soften for a few hours to soak. Put the onion, parsley, bay leaf, marjoram, allspice, pepper, mushrooms and cover with water in a saucepan. Boil for about 40 minutes. Halfway through cooking add the sausages. Then remove the sausages and odors and add about half of the acid base (*zakwas*) shaking it before pouring. Lower the heat and let it boil for another 10 minutes. Season with salt and pepper. Meanwhile, sauté the diced bacon and boil the eggs. Divide the bacon on the plates, sliced sausages and eggs cut in half or into smaller pieces, cover with the freshly made *żurek* and serve hot and with slices of bread.

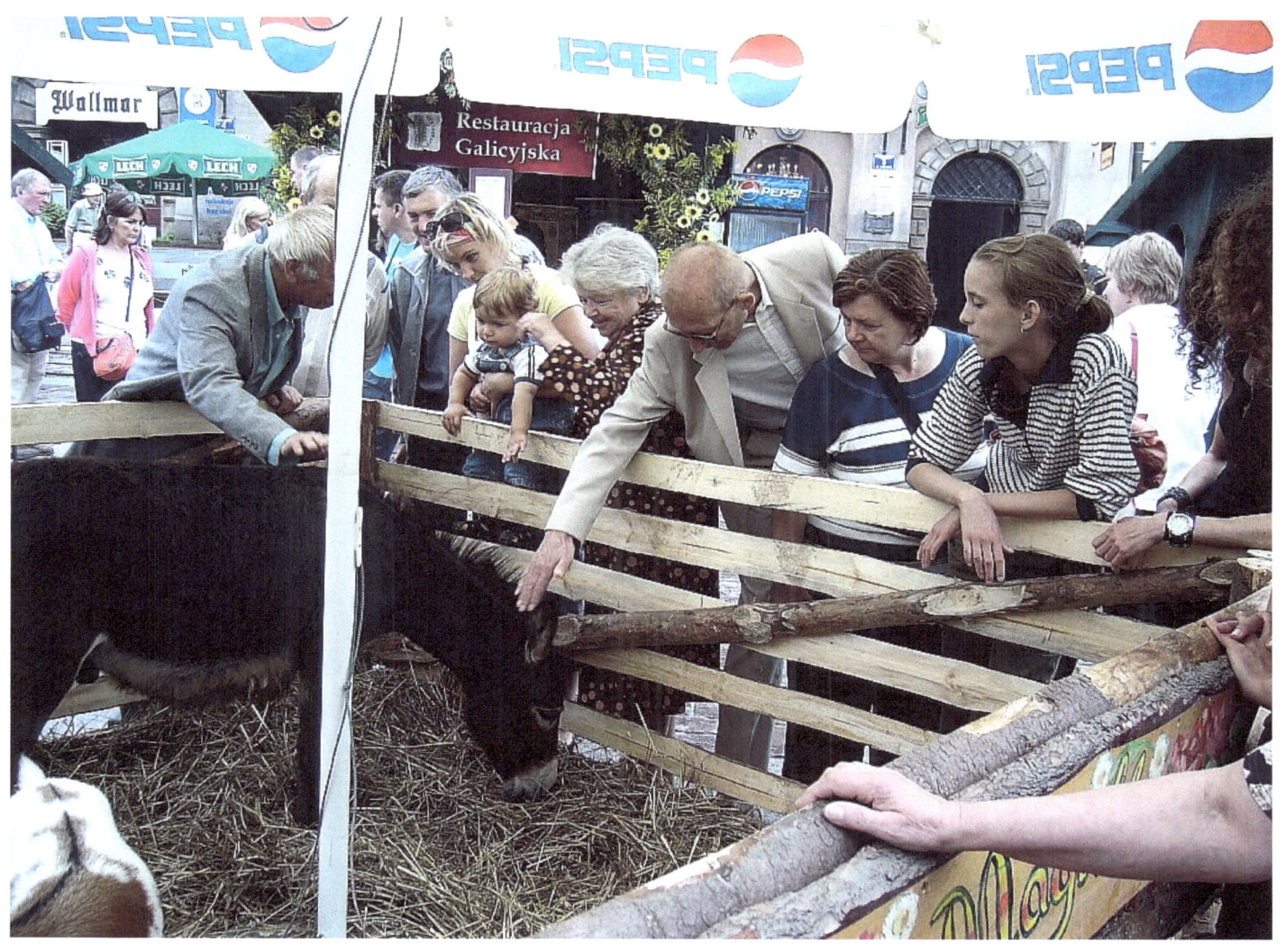

Pierogi, stuffed dumplings. Put the potatoes to boil, knead 2 glasses of flour with the salt, the egg and the oil, adding a little at a time hot water until a soft dough is obtained. Once the potatoes are cooked and cooled, peel and mash with a potato masher. Brown the finely chopped onion and add to the potatoes. Add salt, pepper and salty ricotta (or other soft cheese) and mix all the ingredients well. Roll out the dough until it is about 4 mm thick and make circles with a glass. In the center of each, put a spoonful of stuffing, closing the edges well so that they do not open during cooking…

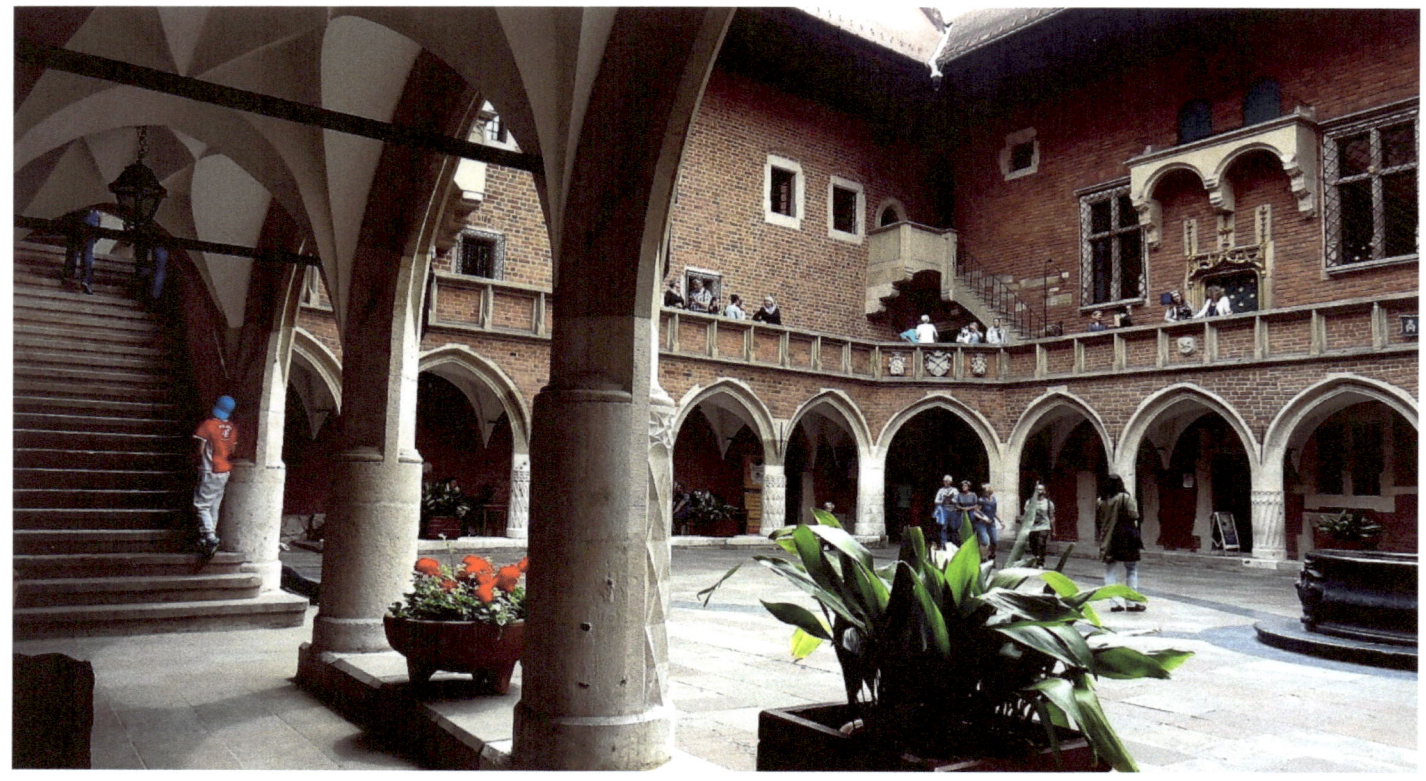

…Cook the *pierogi* in plenty of salted water for about 5 minutes and when they come to the surface drain them and serve hot with the condiment of your choice. Variants:
- stuffing with *pierogi* with meat: boiled meat in broth, sauteed onion, black pepper, pork lard minced together in the meat grinder
- stuffing with *pierogi* with sauerkraut and mushrooms: sauerkraut blanched with forest mushrooms, sauteed onion, pepper, salt)

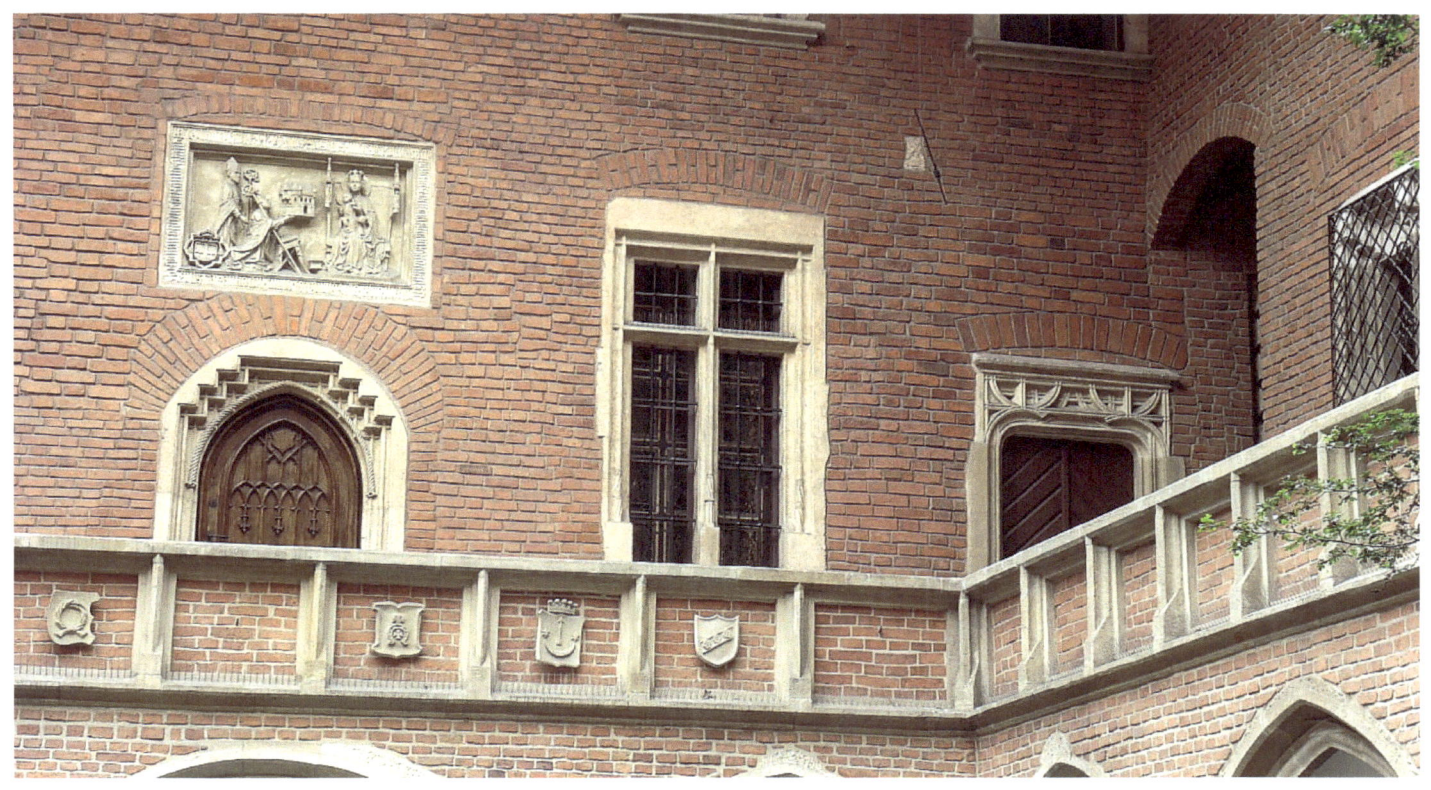

Zupa grzybowa, porcini mushroom soup. Wash the dried mushrooms and let soak for at least 2 hours, then cook in the same water for 20 minutes. Drain and keep the water.

Put a liter and a half of water on the stove, add the carrots and celery cleaned and cut into small pieces, the garlic, the nut and boil for about 30 minutes. Meanwhile, cut the mushrooms into small pieces, chop the onion and brown them on the pan with a little oil. Then add the mushrooms and the onion to the broth, add the peeled potatoes, washed and cut into cubes, the remaining water or at least half in which you cooked the mushrooms and bring everything to boil. At the end pour the cream or yogurt or cheese and mix well. Adjust the soup with salt and pepper. Before serving, sprinkle with chopped parsley.

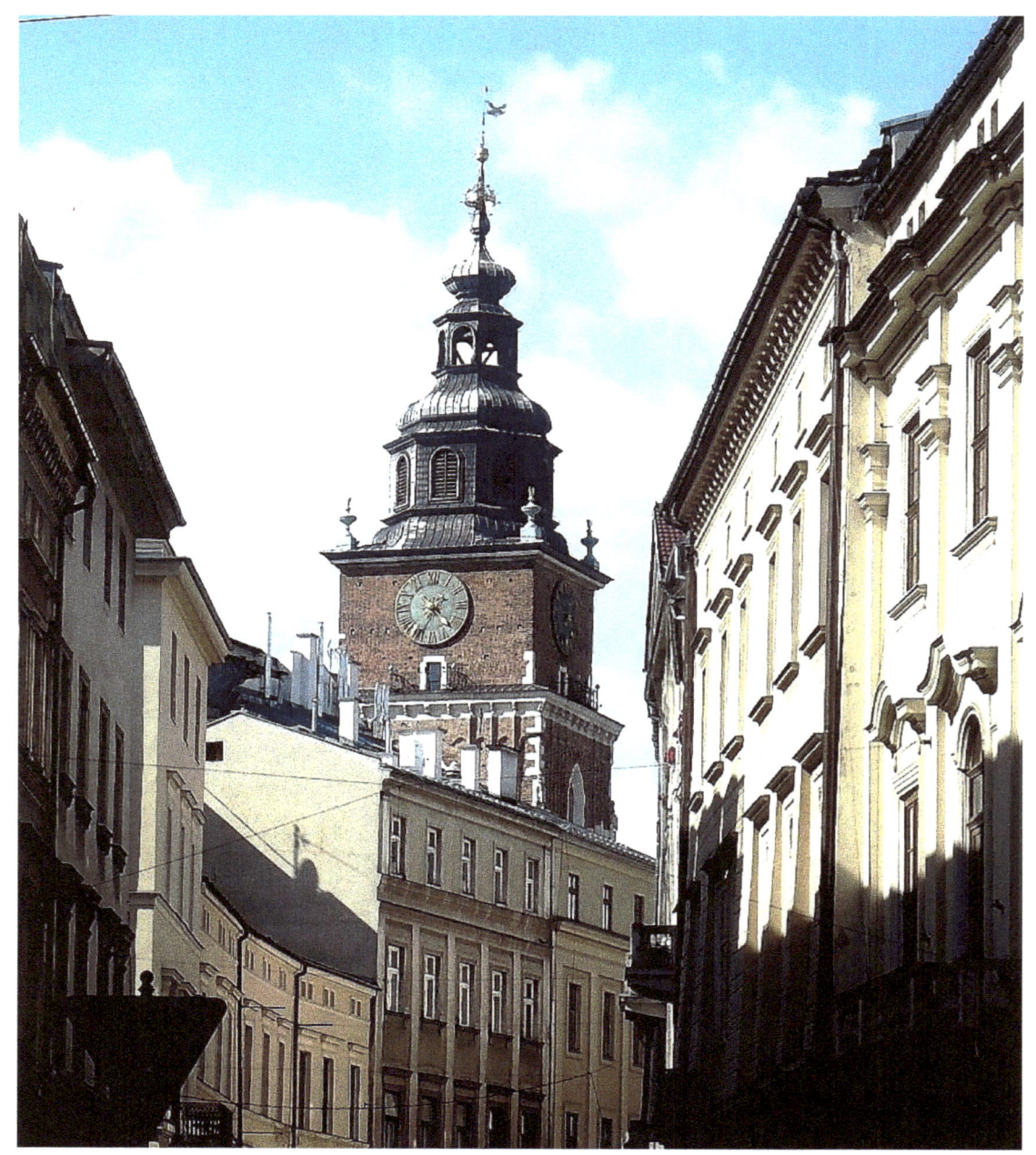

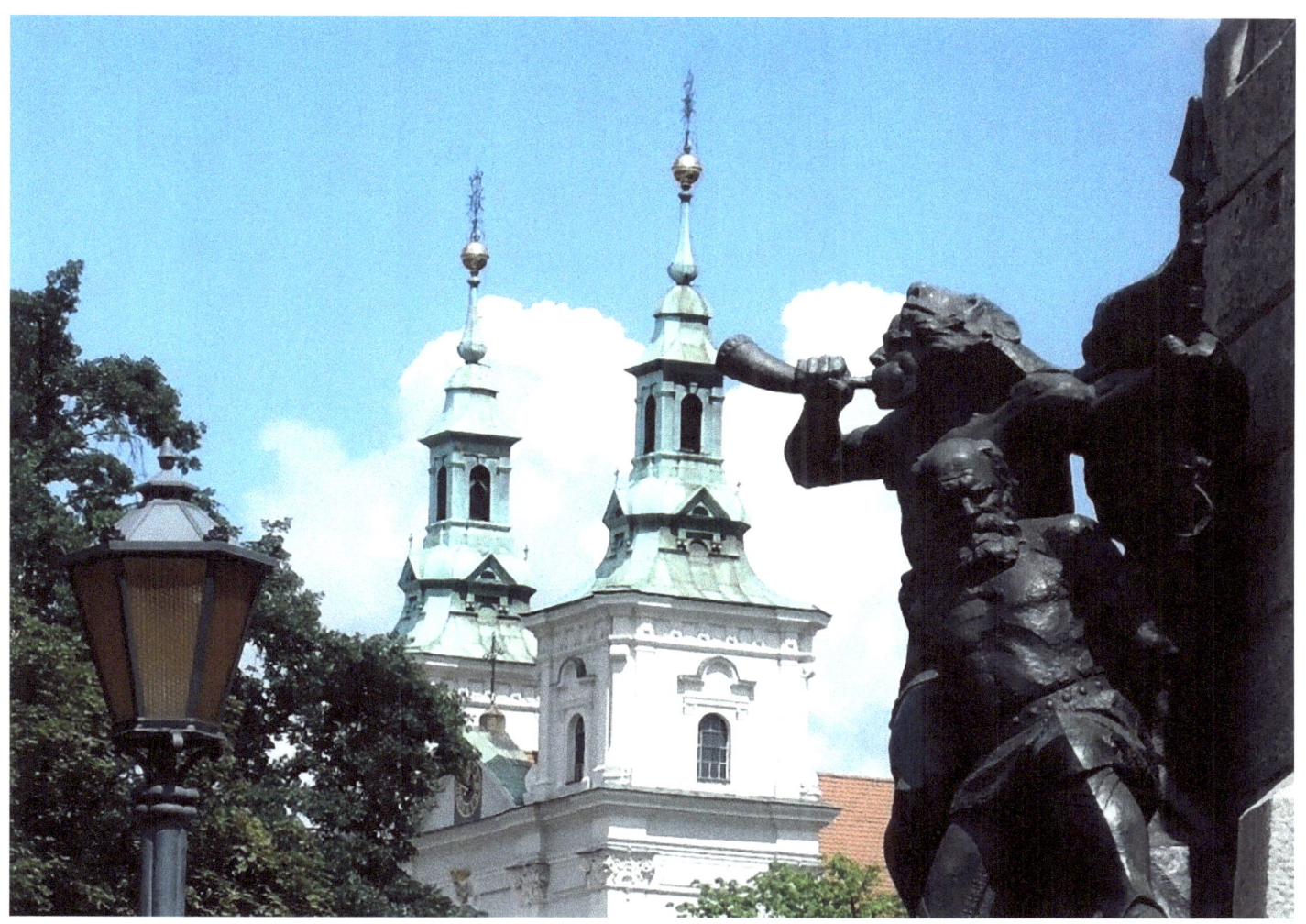

Ogórkowa, soup with sour cucumbers and potatoes. Rinse the pickled cucumbers and cut them into julienne strips, peel the potatoes and cut into cubes. Heat the butter in a pan, add an onion and just starts to brown add the crushed garlic, stirring over low heat for 5 minutes. Add the cucumbers and brown for a few minutes. Pour the broth and add the potatoes. Cook over low heat until the potatoes become soft. Mix 2 tablespoons of white flour with sour cream (or yogurt) and pour the mixture into the soup, stirring carefully to avoid lumps. Let the soup cook for a few minutes, but do not let it boil. Salt and pepper.

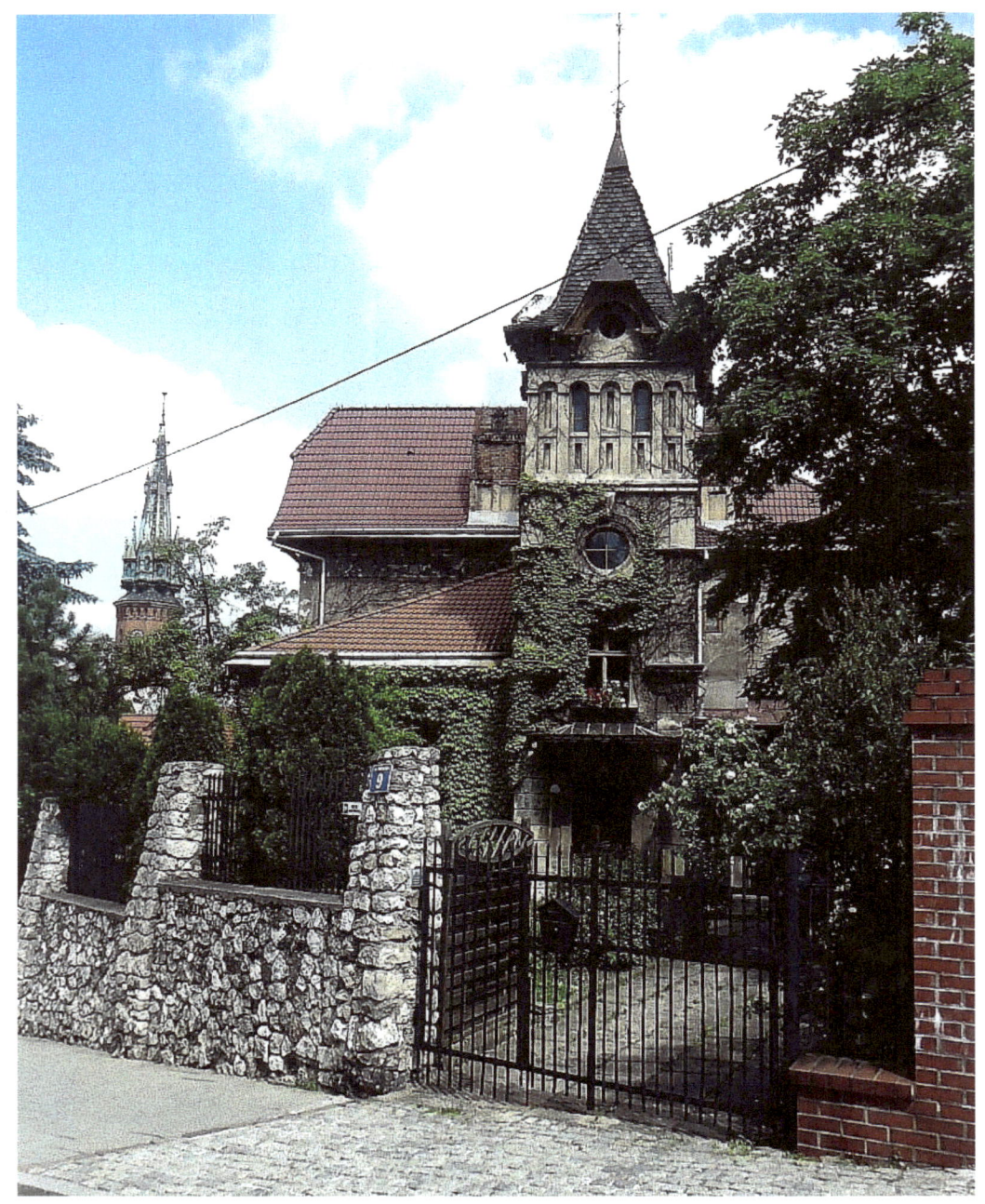

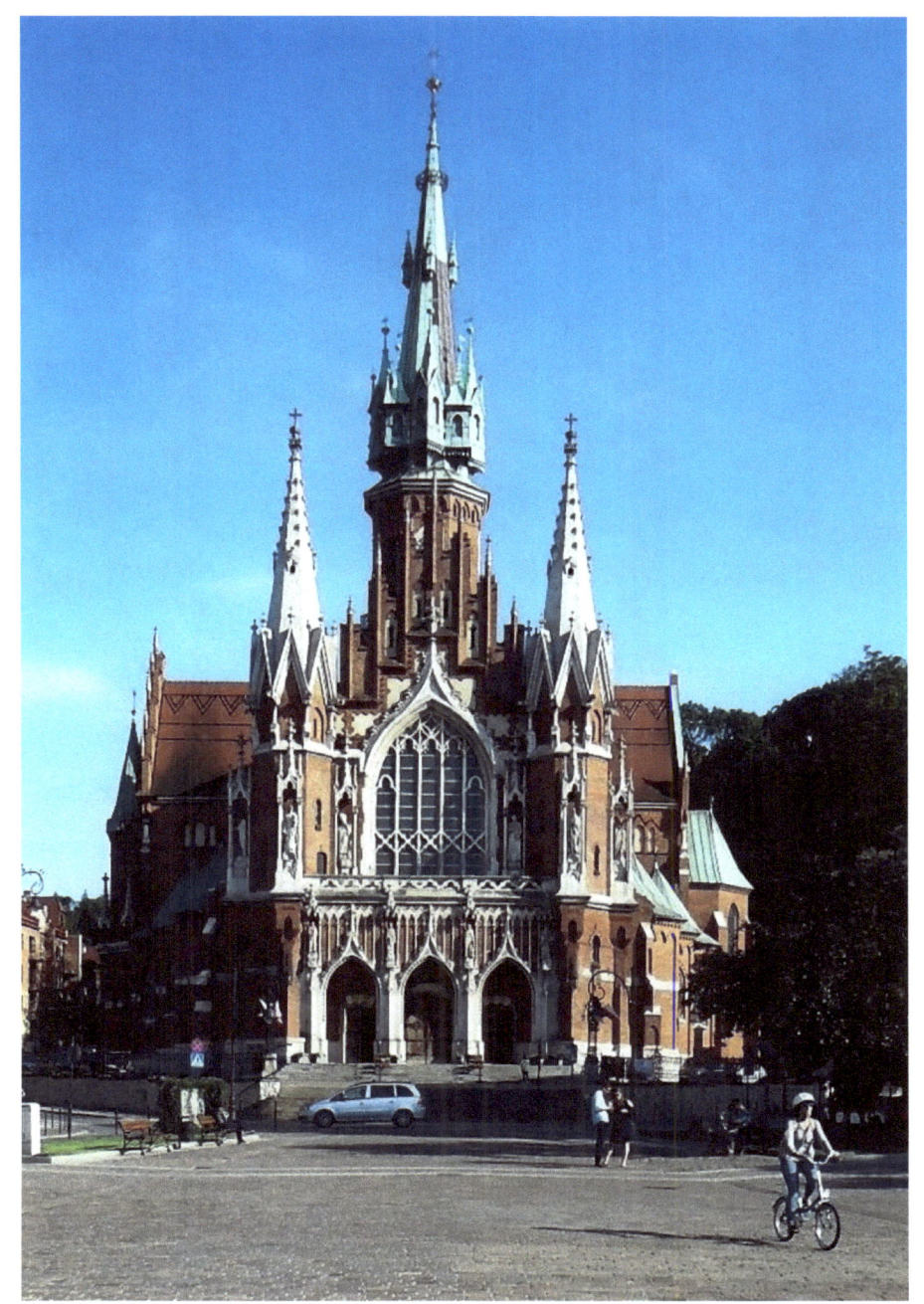

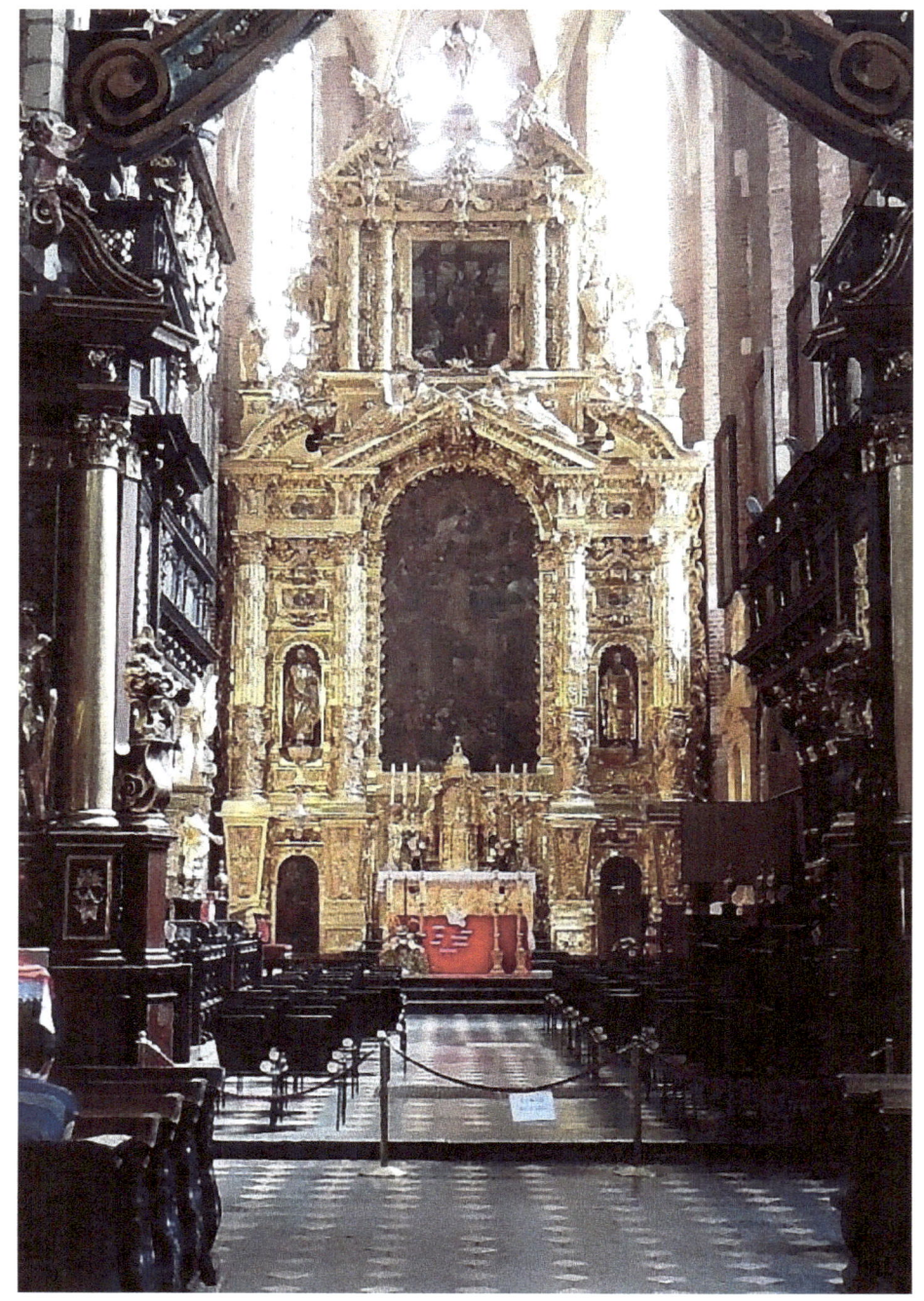

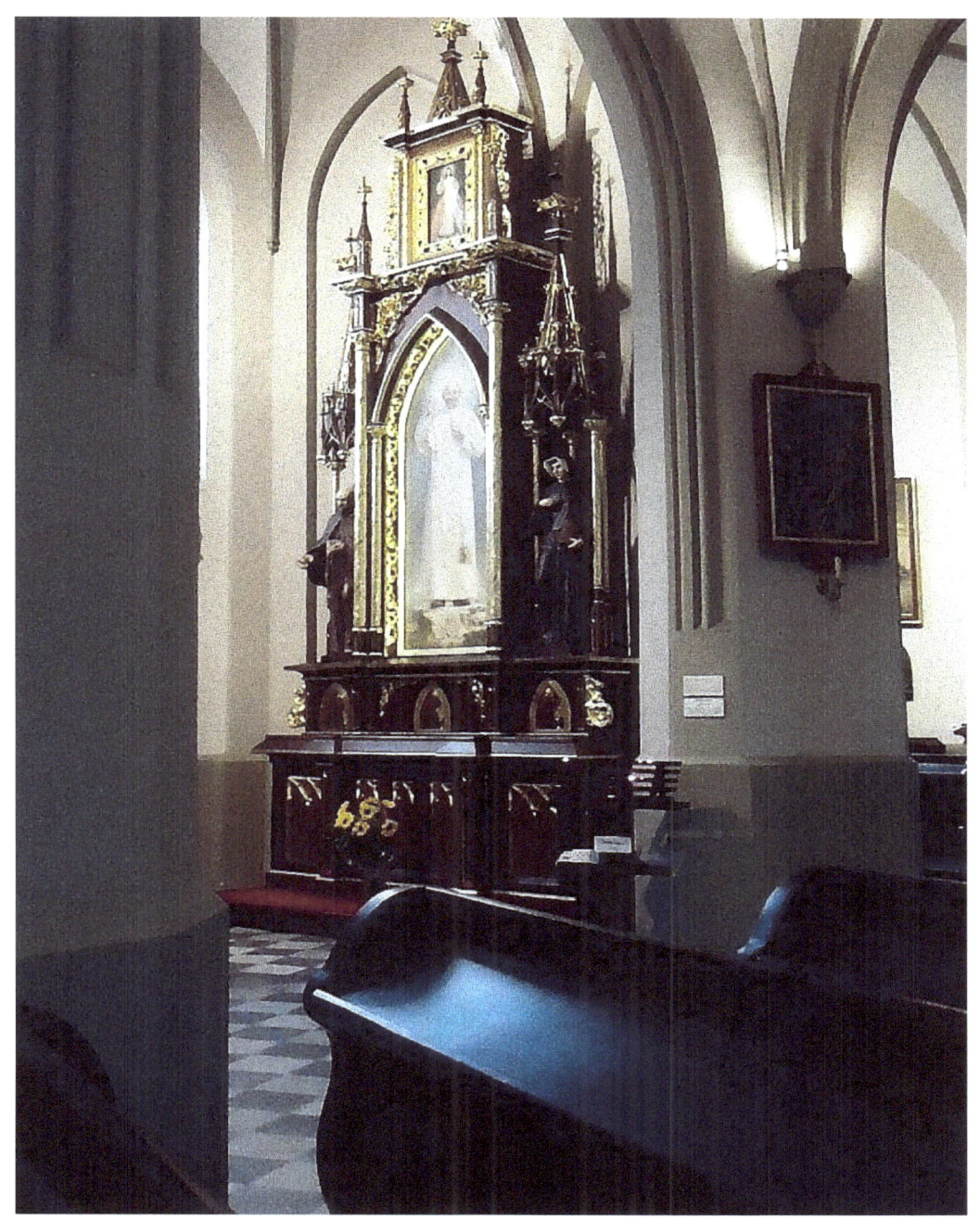

39

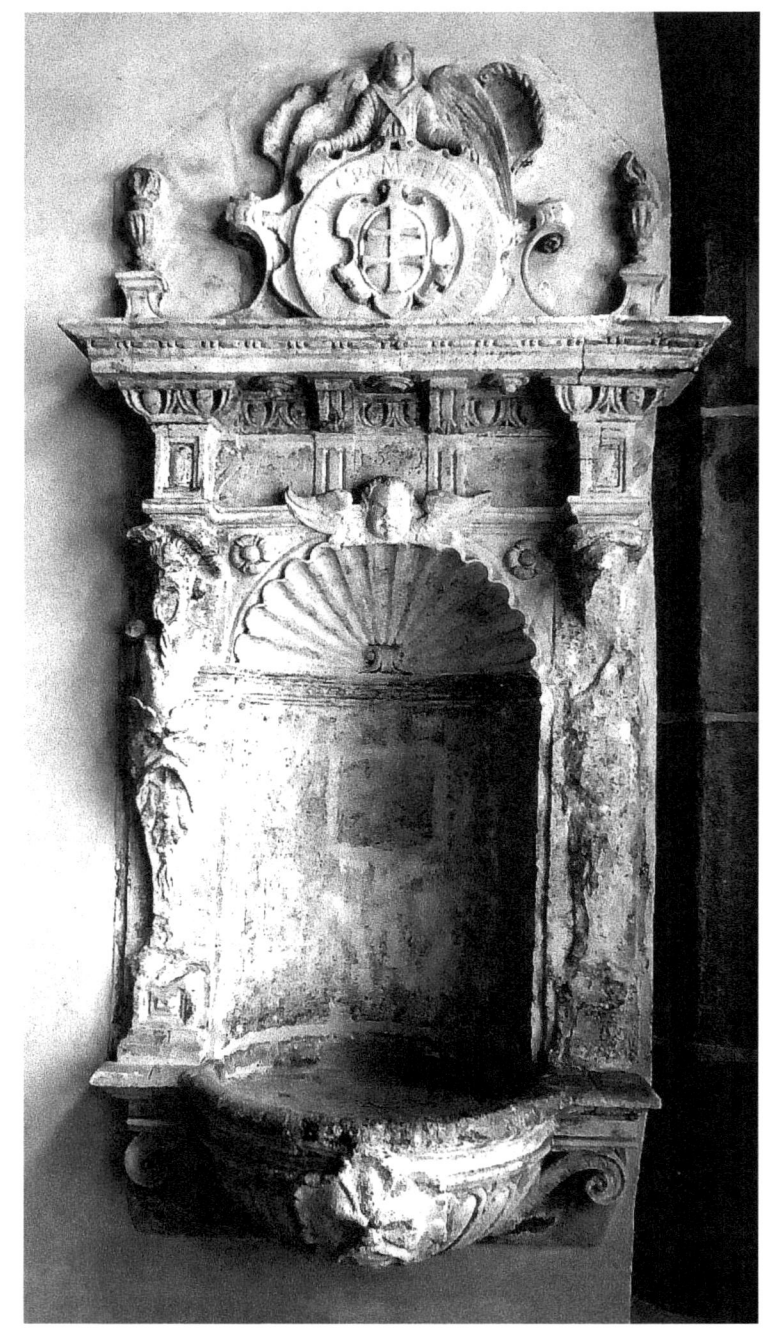

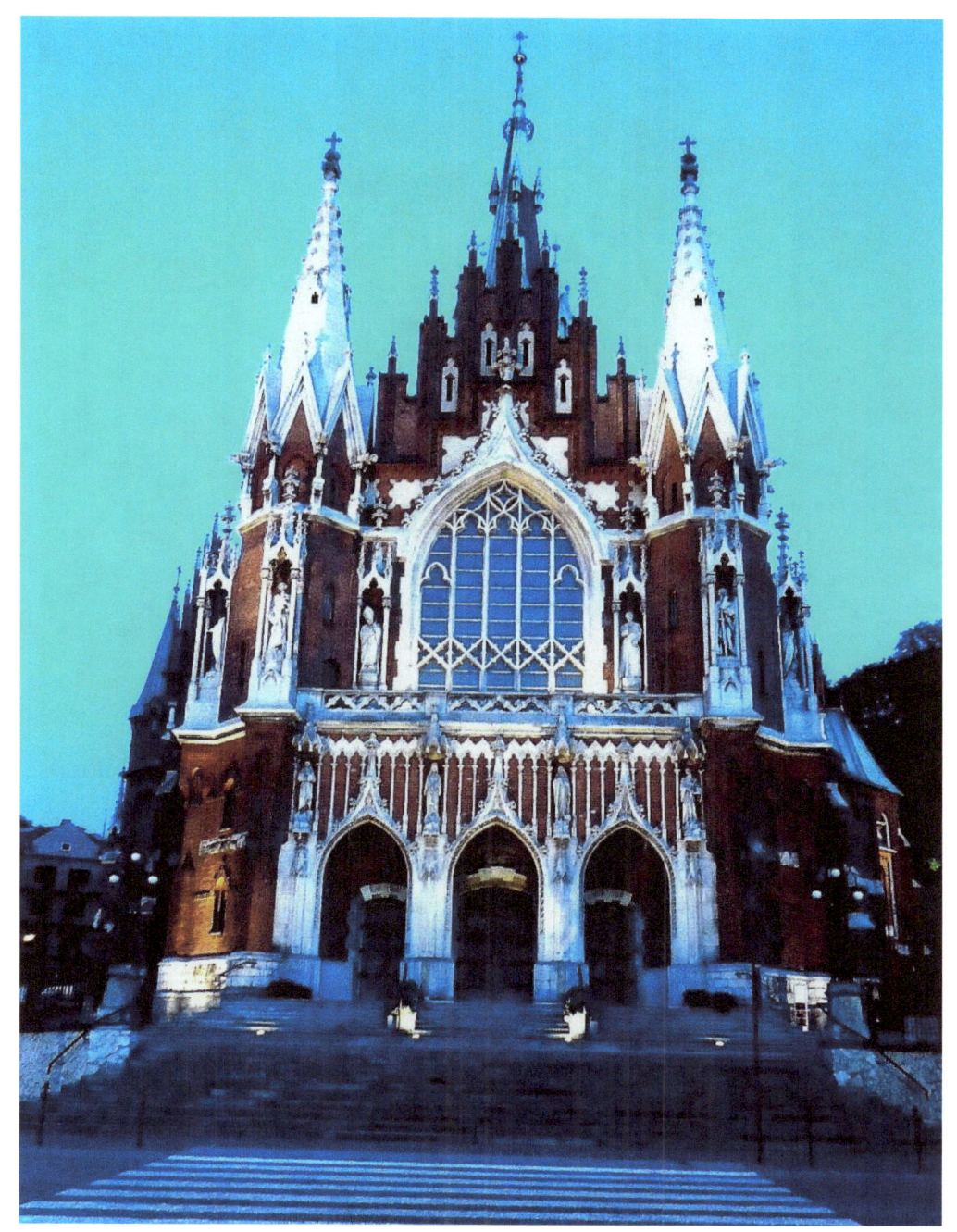

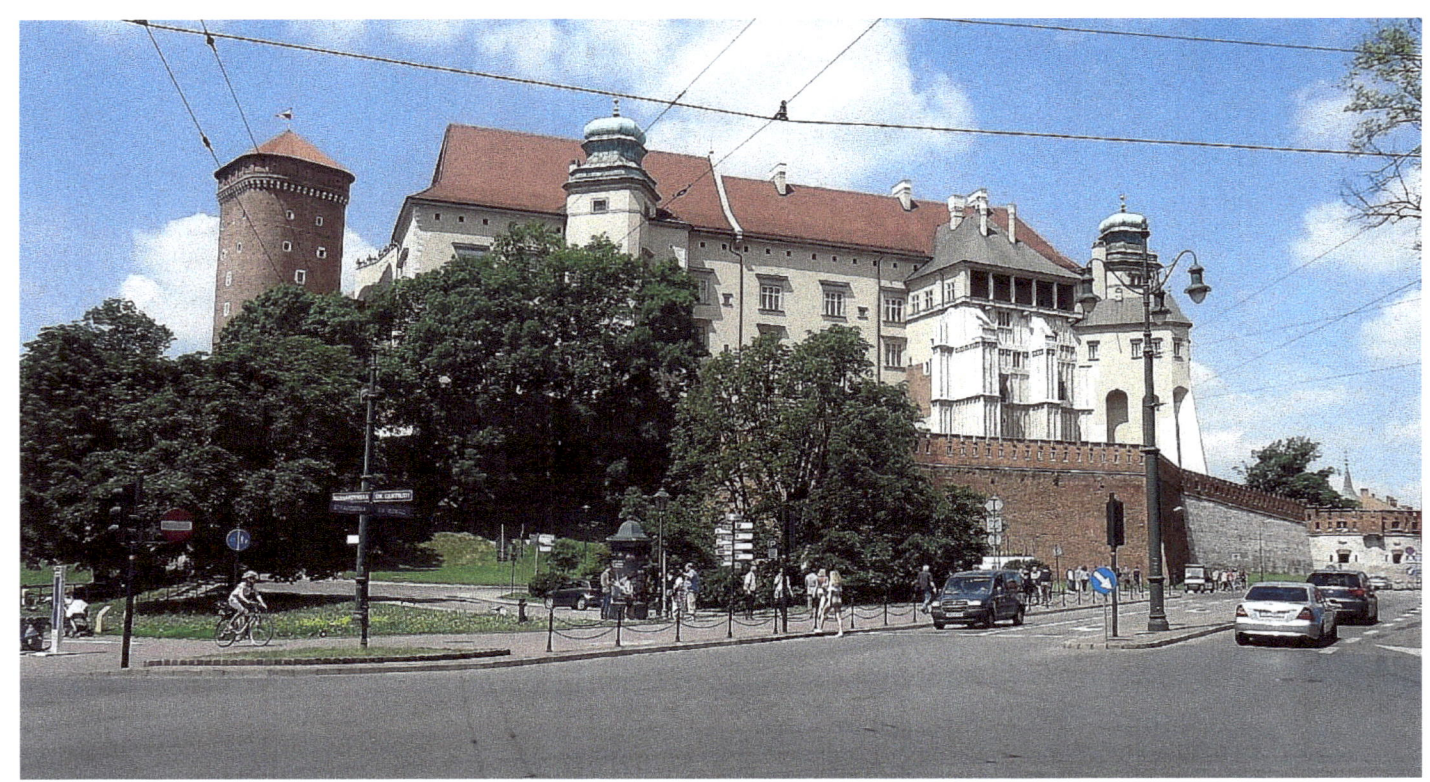

Pyzy, stuffed potato gnocchi. Peel and wash the potatoes. Grate half of them and boil those that remain and pass in a potato masher. Add an egg, some flour, a pinch of salt and the grated potatoes. Grind and brown the beef with sage, onion, walnuts, breadcrumbs, salt and pepper in a pan. From the same cut of meat obtain into slices and brown them in a pan with butter and sage. Form the gnocchi by crushing the potato dough with your hands, insert a little 'stuffing and form a ball. Cook them in plenty of salted water and remove when they come to the surface. Arrange the slices of meat on the plates, place the gnocchi and the valerian sauce seasoned with oil, salt and walnut kernels.

Golonka, pork knuckle. Wash the pork shins, boil them in vegetable stock (over low heat) for 90 minutes with the addition of carrots, bay leaves, black pepper balls and other flavorings to taste. Put the pork shanks in a heat-resistant dish and brush with a syrup of beer, honey and spices. Bake for 120 minutes at 190 C, pouring the beer from the plate every 10 minutes.

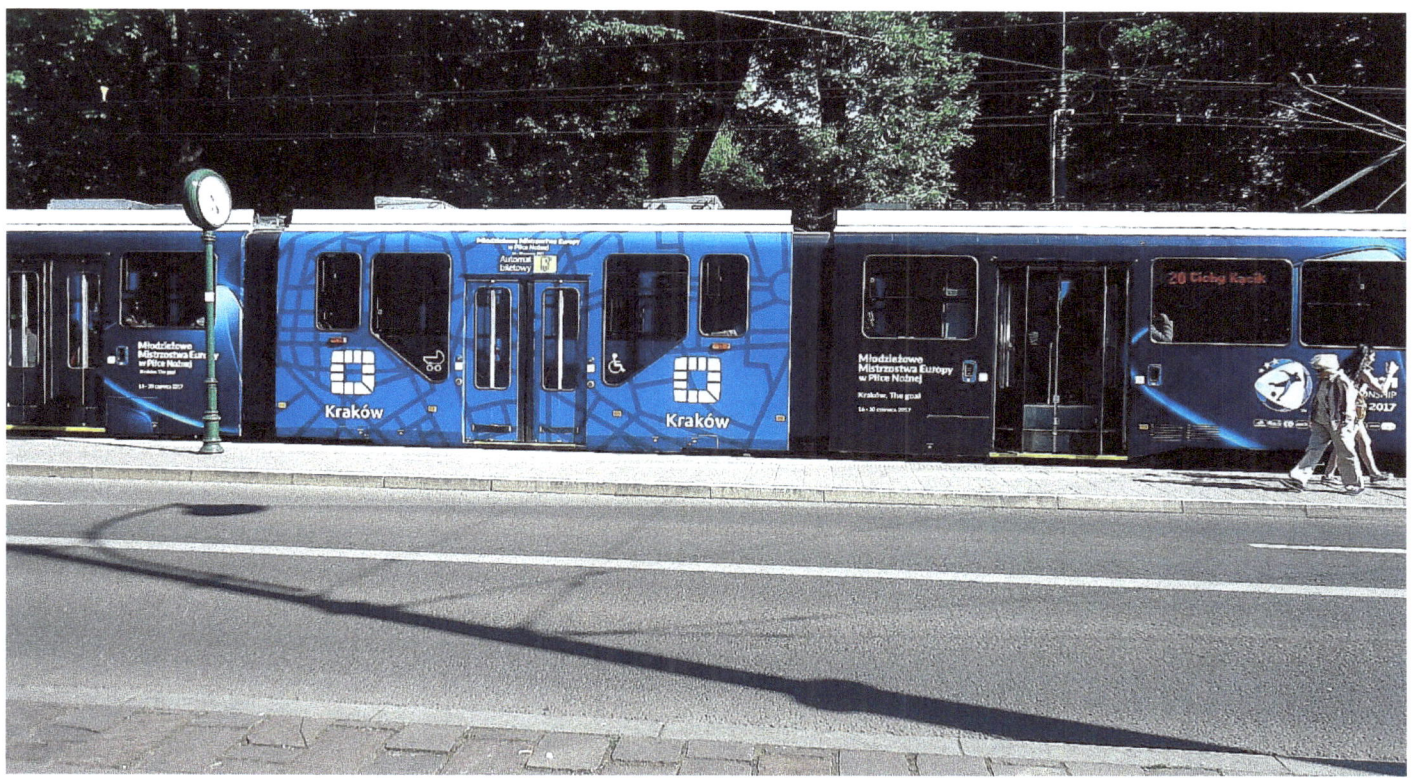

Bigos. Rinse the dried mushrooms and let soften in hot water. Drain the sauerkraut, chop into smaller pieces then add 2 water glasses and cook for about half an hour. Chop, rinse and cook the cabbage for about half an hour. Cut the cooked pork into small pieces, slice the sausages and chop the onion. Cut the bacon into cubes and fry without adding other greases (without oil or butter). Then add the meat, sausage and onion and cook all the ingredients for a few minutes. If necessary, add a little water. In the same pot where the sauerkraut is cooked, add the mushrooms cut in half, then the cabbage and the meat already cooked separately. Add the aromas (juniper, bay leaf, pimento, marjoram) and cook over a low heat for more than an hour, stirring and adding wine occasionally. At the end of cooking add a little 'tomato and adjust with salt and pepper.

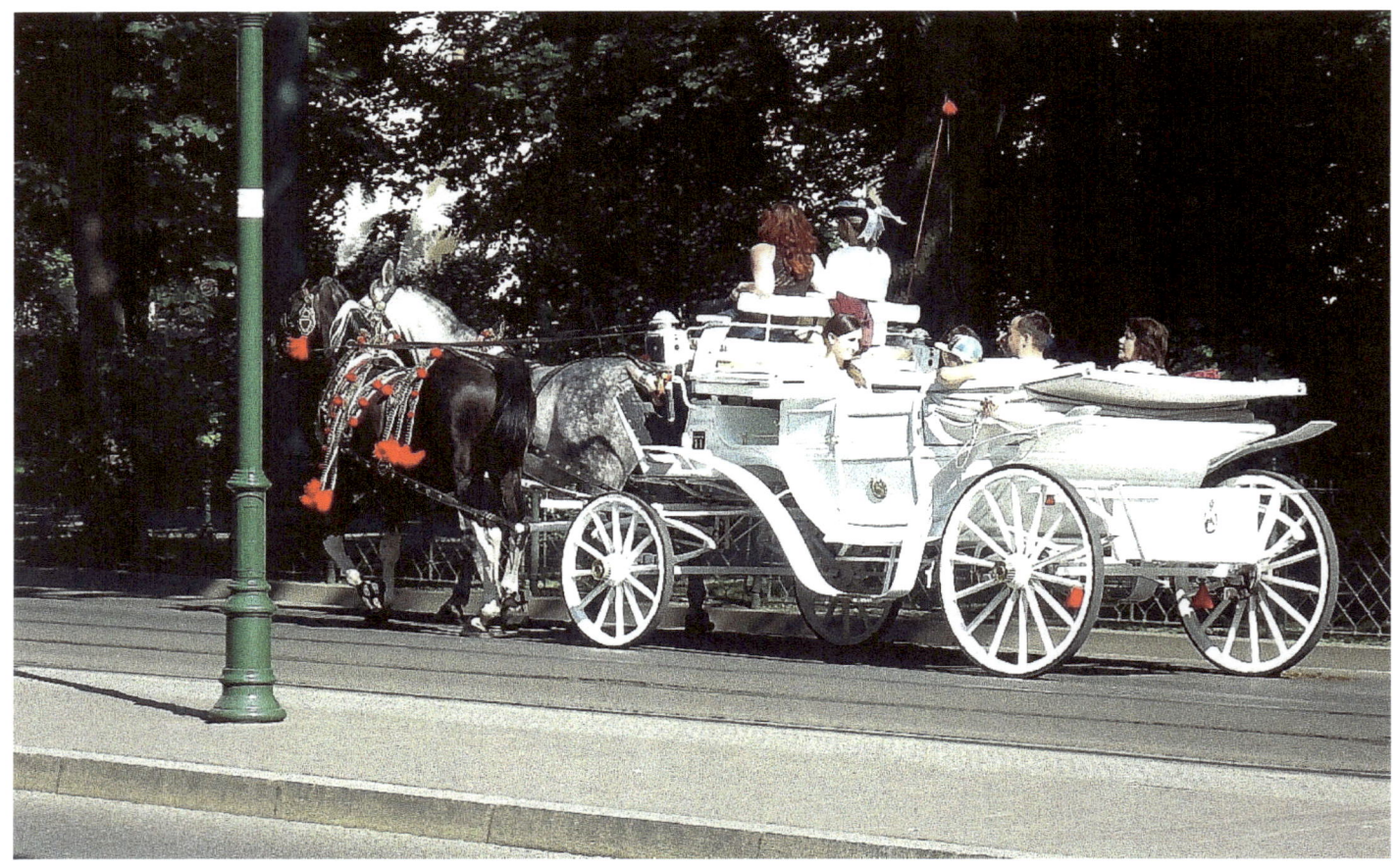

Filet z jagnięciny, lamb fillet. Salt and pepper the slices of lamb fillet and brown in a pan over high heat for 4 minutes on each side with a little oil already hot. Remove them from the container and keep warm. Melt the butter in a saucepan, add the chopped onion and brown. Drain the mushrooms from their preserving liquid, drain well and cut into 4 parts. Throw them in the saucepan and let simmer for a few minutes, then season with salt, white pepper and paprika. Lastly the minced parsley. Stir well and remove the saucepan from the heat. Wash the tomatoes and make a cross cut on top of each.

In another saucepan, melt the remaining butter and place the tomatoes on top and heat for 3 minutes over high heat. Then toast the slices of white bread and place on a hot serving dish. Arrange on top of the fillet slices kept warm, spread a portion of the mushrooms on each slice, garnish with the tomatoes warmed in butter and serve immediately hot.

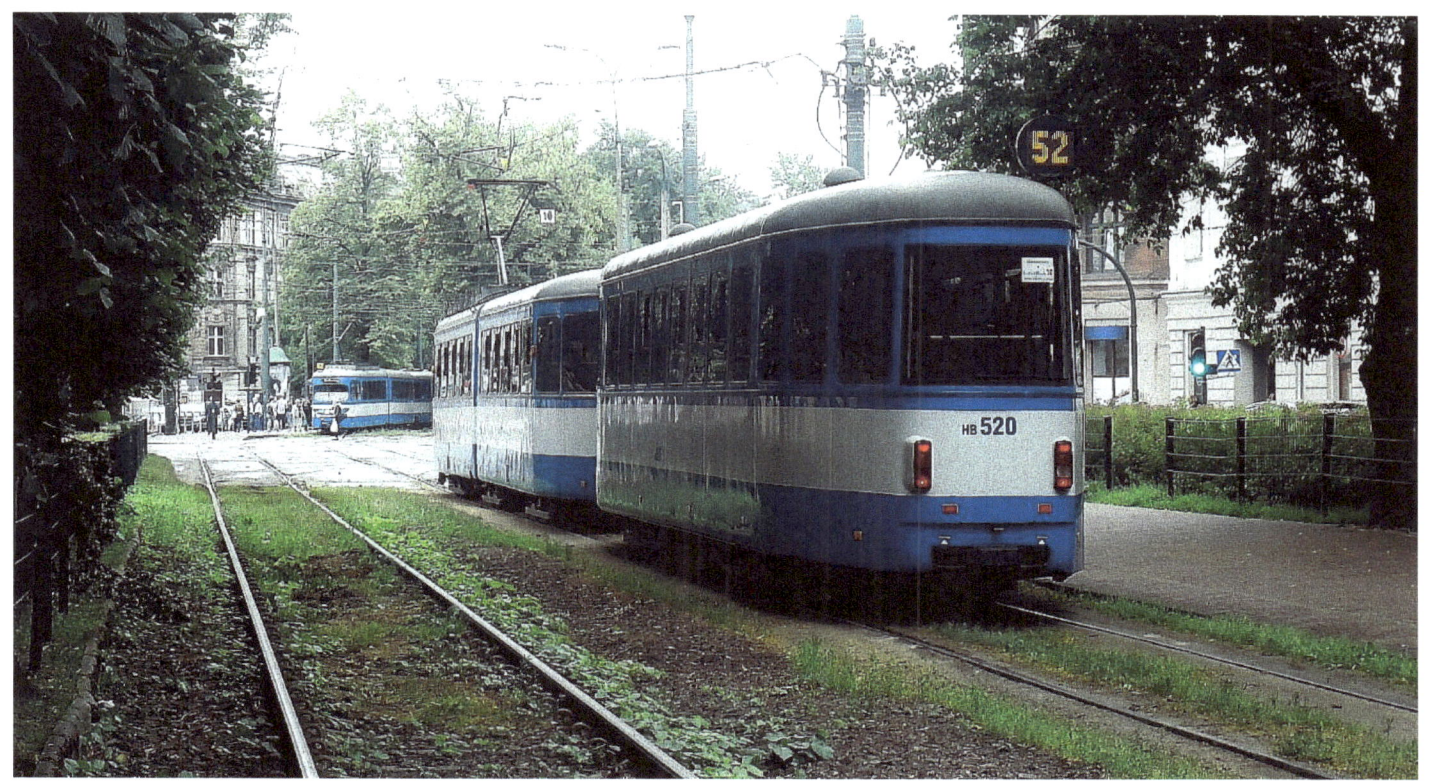

Gulasz wolowy, beef gulash. Cut the beef shoulder into large cubes, flour them and fry thoroughly in hot oil, then place in a large pot. In the same frying pan of the meat fry the diced onions and at the end add the diced red and green peppers and the peeled garlic cloves. Dilute the tomato paste with a little water and pour into a pan. Add the sweet paprika, the ground pepper, the bay leaves, the pimento, the cumin and pour everything into the large pot with the fried beef cubes. Cover the ingredients with meat broth and cook on medium gas with a lid for a maximum of 3 hours, stirring occasionally and filling the evaporated liquid. When cooked, salt and pepper. If the sauce is too diluted, you can thicken with a batter of water and flour.

Smazony boczek z suszona sliwka, fried bacon with prunes. The slice of bacon is rolled around a dried plum and stopped with a toothpick. The preparation is roasted for a few moments on a pan and served hot.

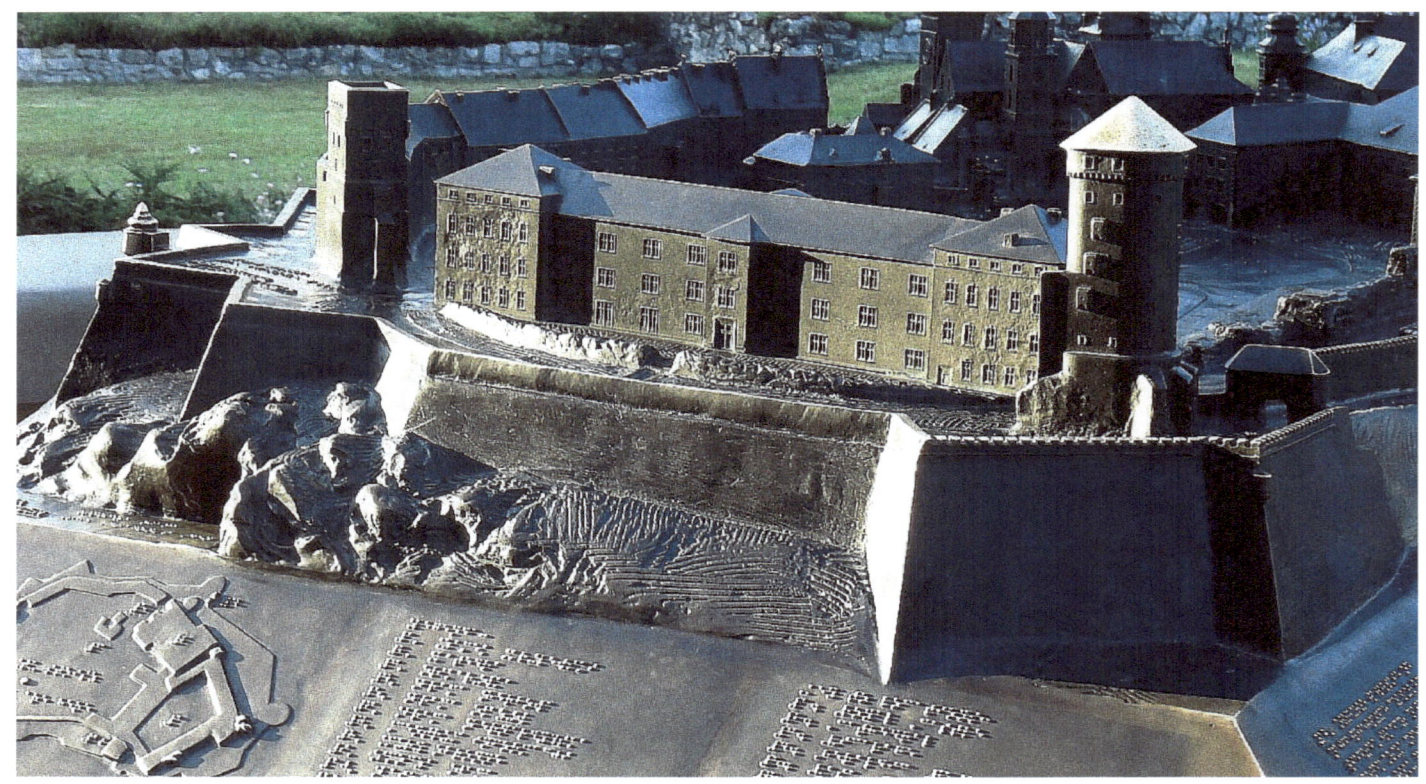

Język polski, Polish tongue. Wash the beef tongue under running water, place it in a saucepan, add the water, a pinch of salt and let it cook for 2 ½ hours in a covered container. When 20 minutes are left at the end of cooking, prepare the sauce by reviving the raisins in hot water and letting it drain well. Put it in a saucepan with the almonds, the grated lemon peel and the red wine and cook for 10 minutes on a moderate heat. Remove a quarter liter from the cooking broth and filter it. Melt the margarine in a saucepan, add the flour and let it brown for 5 minutes, stirring constantly. Dilute with the broth filtered and continue cooking for 5 minutes, stirring well. Grate the panpepato, add it to the sauce, bring to a boil for a moment, then add the mixture of wine with raisins, almonds and lemon peel. Season with vinegar, sugar, a pinch of salt and a pinch of pepper. Finally add the butter and mix everything until the butter has melted completely. Then keep the sauce warm. Remove the tongue from the cooking broth, peel, removing the ossicles and small cartilages that are in the thickest part and cut into slices of a half centimeter thick. Arrange the slices on a heated dish, pour over the hot sauce and serve immediately.

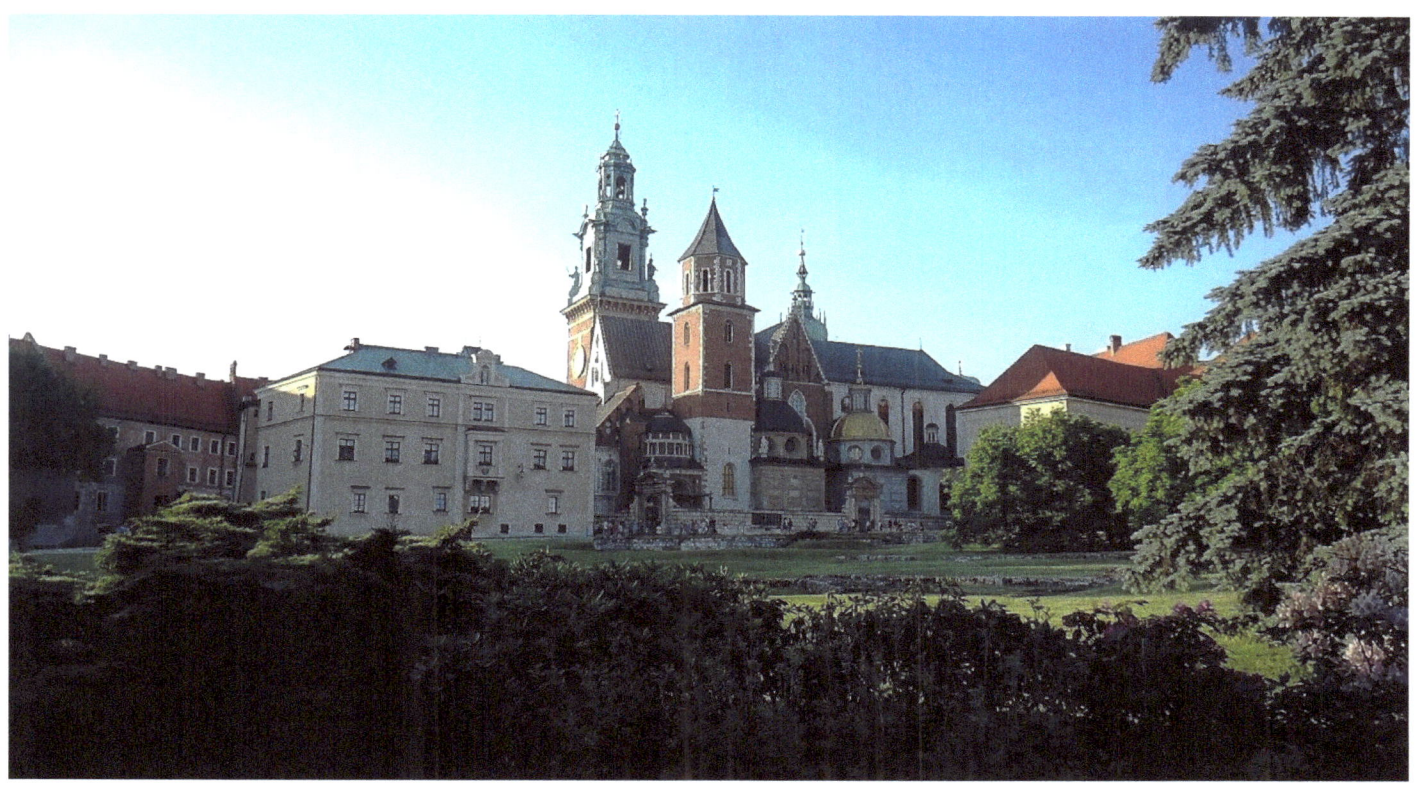

Zrazy, beef roll. Cut a piece of beef so that on one side it remains attached for only a few centimeters. Then salt, pepper internally and externally and brush on the inside with a light layer of mustard. Then roll the meat on itself and wrap in aluminum foil.

Stuffing: melt the butter in a pan, put in the finely chopped onions and let them brown. Sprinkle over the breadcrumbs and brown mixing them for 5 minutes. Stir in a bowl the fried breadcrumbs and onion with the minced parsley and the egg, salt and pepper the filling and season with the nutmeg. Roll out the meat, spread over the filling and roll it back on itself, tying with some thread. Cut the lard into cubes, toast them in a large saucepan and then remove with the skimmer. Place the roll of meat in the hot grease and let it brown for 10 minutes on all sides. Cut the bacon and diced onions and after 7 minutes of cooking add to the meat, then sprinkle with chopped parsley, chervil and tarragon. Wet the meat with the red wine and the stock broth and let cook for an hour and a half over a moderate flame in a covered container.

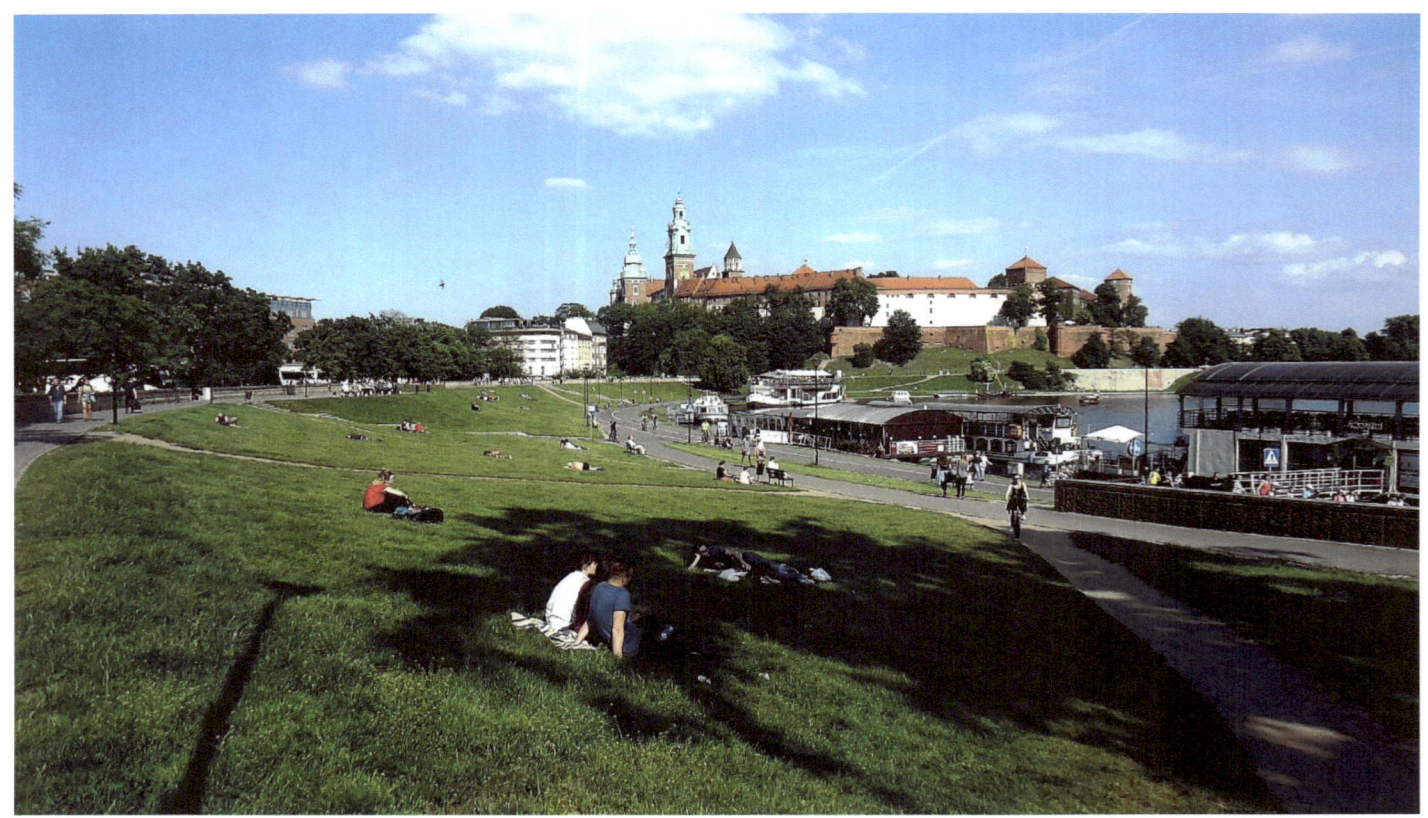

Gołąbki, cabbage rolls. Soften the leaves of a large cabbage in boiling salted water. Stuffing: brown a finely chopped onion in a knob of butter and chop it with half a kilo of veal, a little less pork, a bowl of boiled rice, two eggs and a pinch of salt and pepper. Fill each cabbage leaf with a little of this stuffing and roll up like a roulade that you'll put in a baking dish, layer by layer. Cover the rolls with water and bake at 190° for about two hours. At the end of cooking, take a cup of water, eliminate the remaining one and pour a jar of tomato sauce into the pan. Bake it again for a few minutes until the rolls are soft at the right point. Finally sprinkle with parsley and serve the rolls still warm.

Kapusta, cabbage. Wash and cut a cabbage into small pieces. Boil it in salted water and change the water twice. Add two carrots cut into small pieces and cook. Separately, fry a small finely chopped onion, a clove of garlic and some sausages in a little oil. When the cabbage is cooked, pour it into the pan, add salt and pepper, add the half-lime juice and cook for 15 minutes.

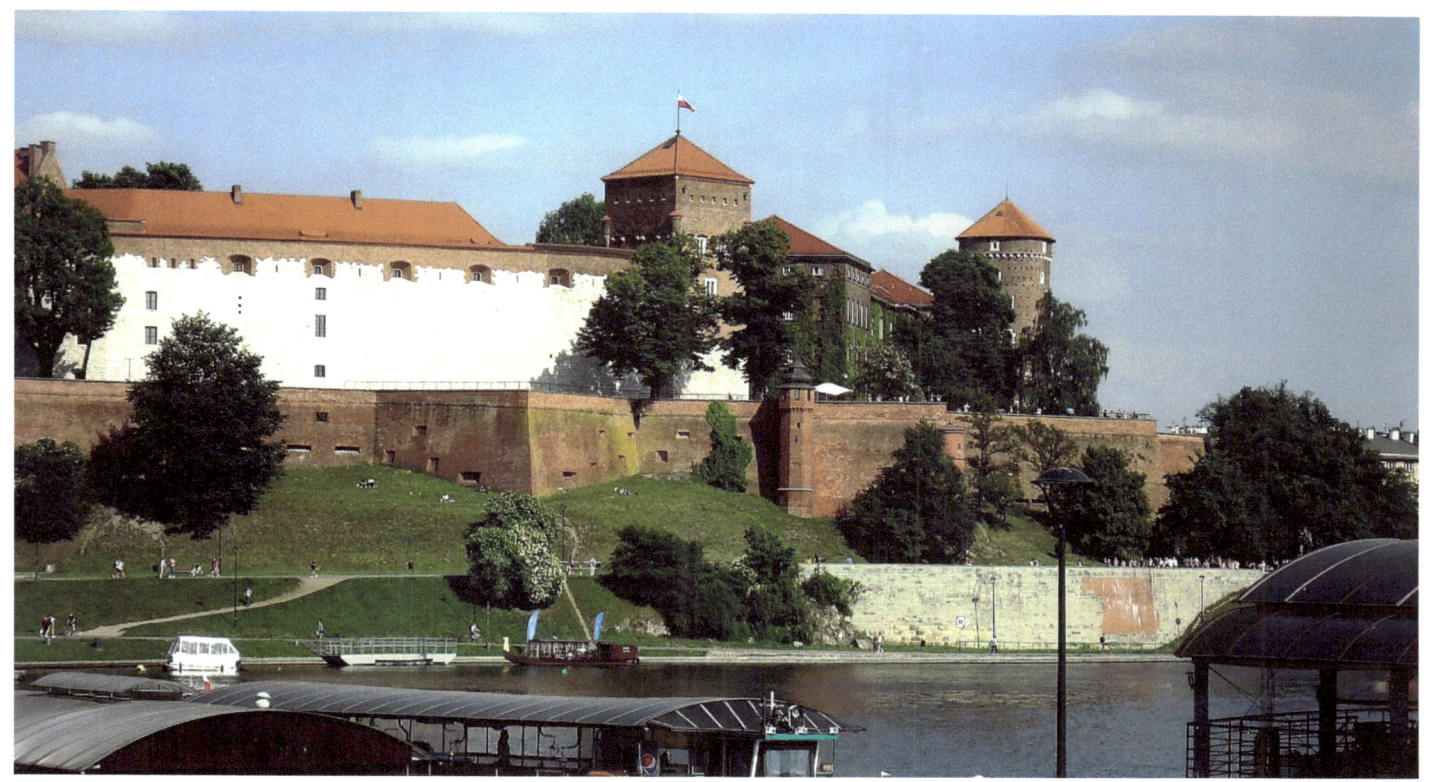

Gotowana sałatka z buraków, hot beetroot salad. Grate the beets and fry them with onion and apple cubes. Add salt, pepper, a little sugar, oil and lemon juice. Fry everything until the mixture is golden.

Leczo, peperonata. Clean and peel the onions, cut them in half and then into wedges. Fry them in a pan with plenty of oil over medium heat with a little water to soften the onions. Wash and dry the peppers, clean them well from the seeds, cut them in half and blanch. Pour a little 'lard (or oil) in a pot rather large, heat it and add the peppers, brown for a few moments and add the fried onions stirring well. If the peppers had to sticking to the pot, add a teaspoon of water. Add two teaspoons of paprika powder and the hot pepper. Season with salt. Blanch the tomatoes, clean them well and cut into large cubes, then add them to the rest. Cut the sausages into slices, add them to the *leczo* and sauté over high heat for two minutes. Cover with the lid and keep on low heat for about thirty minutes. Take care it does not burn.

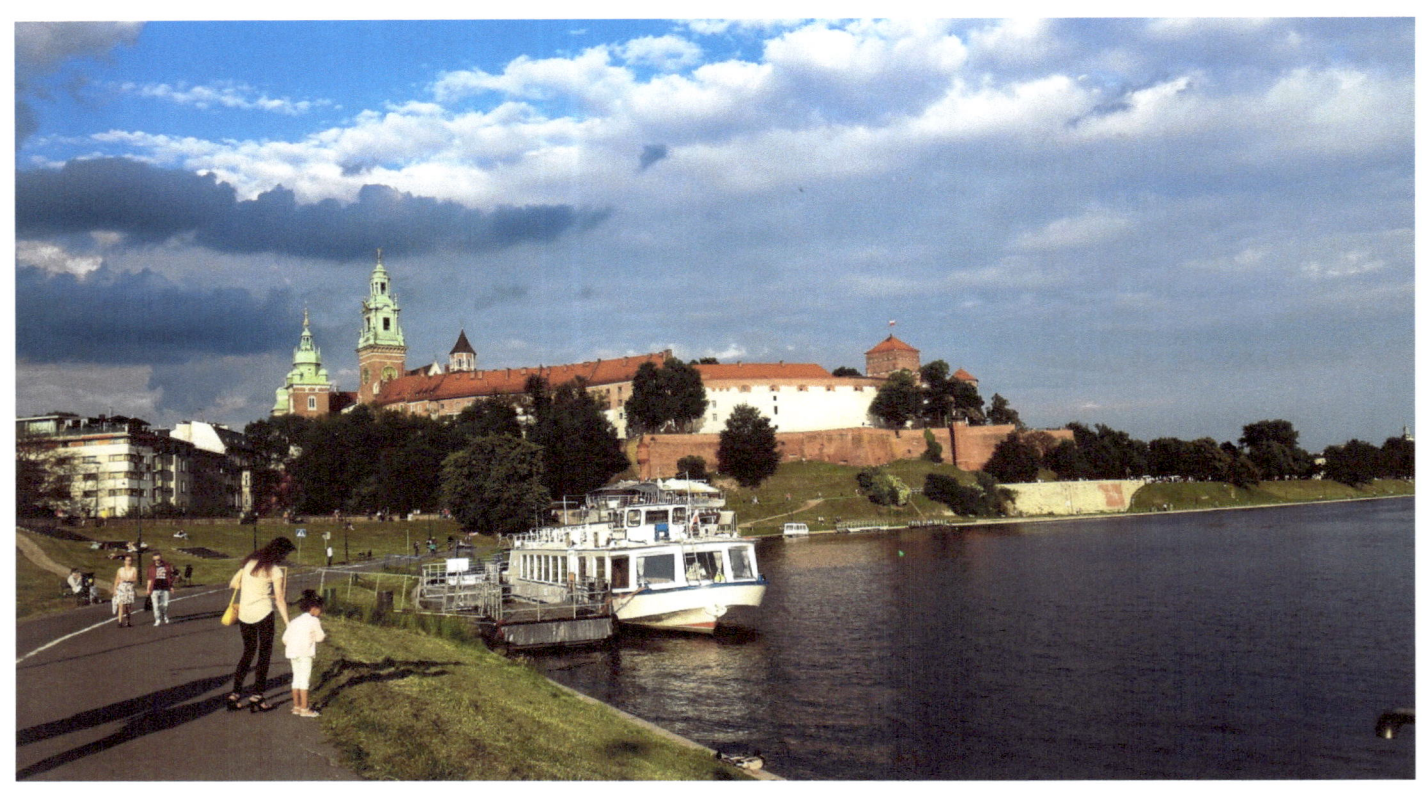

Paszteciki, rustics. Divide half a cabbage to leaves, discarding the hardest parts. Cut them into small pieces and place in boiling water. Let it boil for 3 minutes and drain. Cut the onions into small pieces and sauté them in the margarine. Add the boiled cabbage leaves to the onion and cook for a moment. Meanwhile, cut the Champignons mushrooms and the diced hard-boiled eggs and fry everything in the margarine with the previous mixture. Season with salt and pepper.

Then prepare the dough: dissolve the yeast in the cream and add it to the flour and margarine. Knead and let rise until doubled. Divide it into 4 rolls that you will squash with the rolling pin until you obtain a rectangular dough of one centimeter of thickness. Arrange the filling on the longest side and roll it up by joining the outer edges. Turn the rolls over, leaving the joint below, cut them into 5 cm long portions. and place in a greased pan of margarine. Wanting the rustics can be smeared with a beaten egg to make them golden on the surface. Bake in a hot oven for 25 minutes.

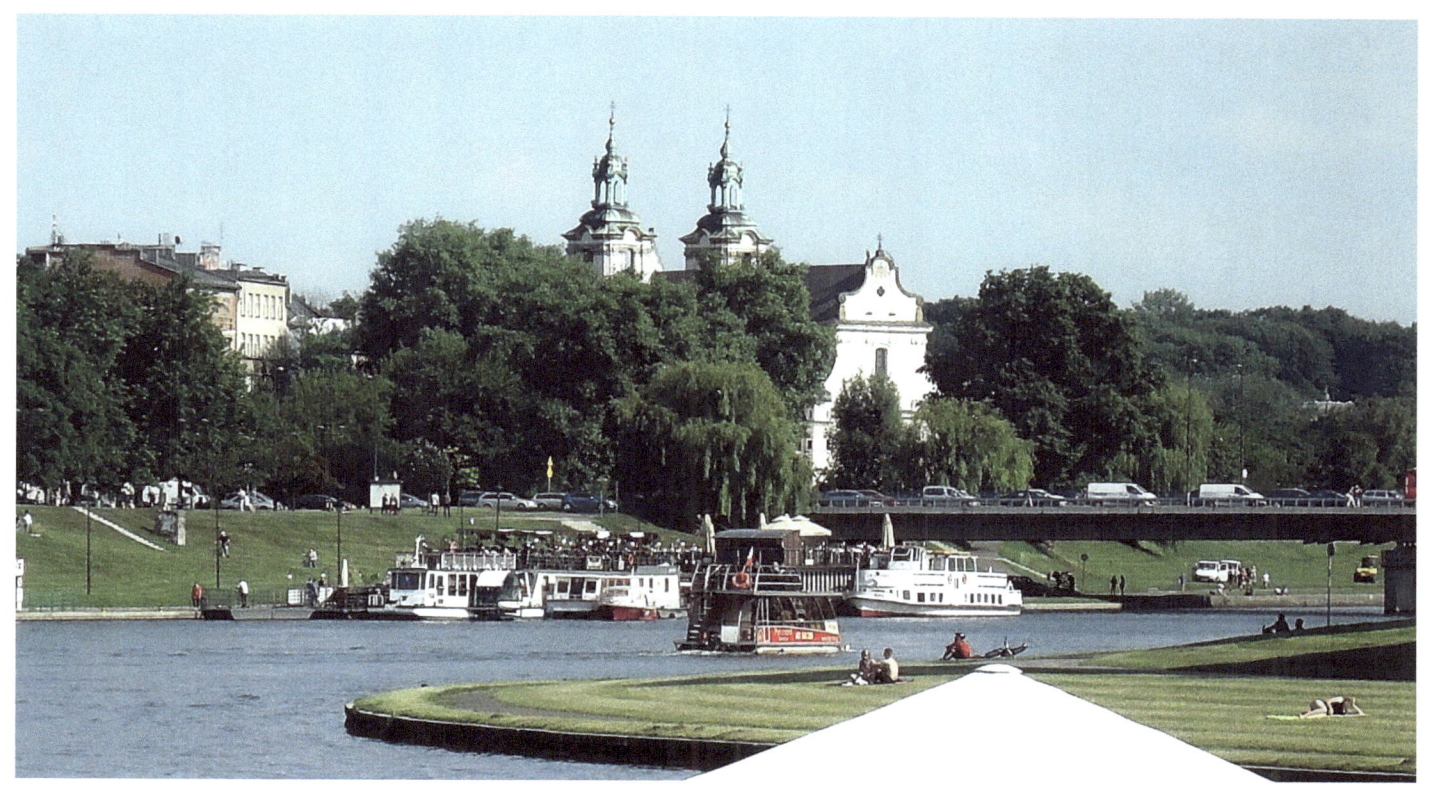

Surowa sałatka z buraków, raw beetroot salad. Grate the beets and apples coarsely, chop the onion and pickled cucumbers, sprinkle with lemon juice and oil, add the cream, stir and sprinkle with chives to taste.

Kalafior, cauliflower. Wash the cauliflower, clean and boil it whole in boiling salted water for 30 minutes. Drain it and place on a hot plate. Lightly brown the butter, add 2 tablespoons of breadcrumbs and the finely chopped hard-boiled egg, leaving it to season for a few minutes. Pour the mixture over the cauliflower and sprinkle with finely chopped parsley.

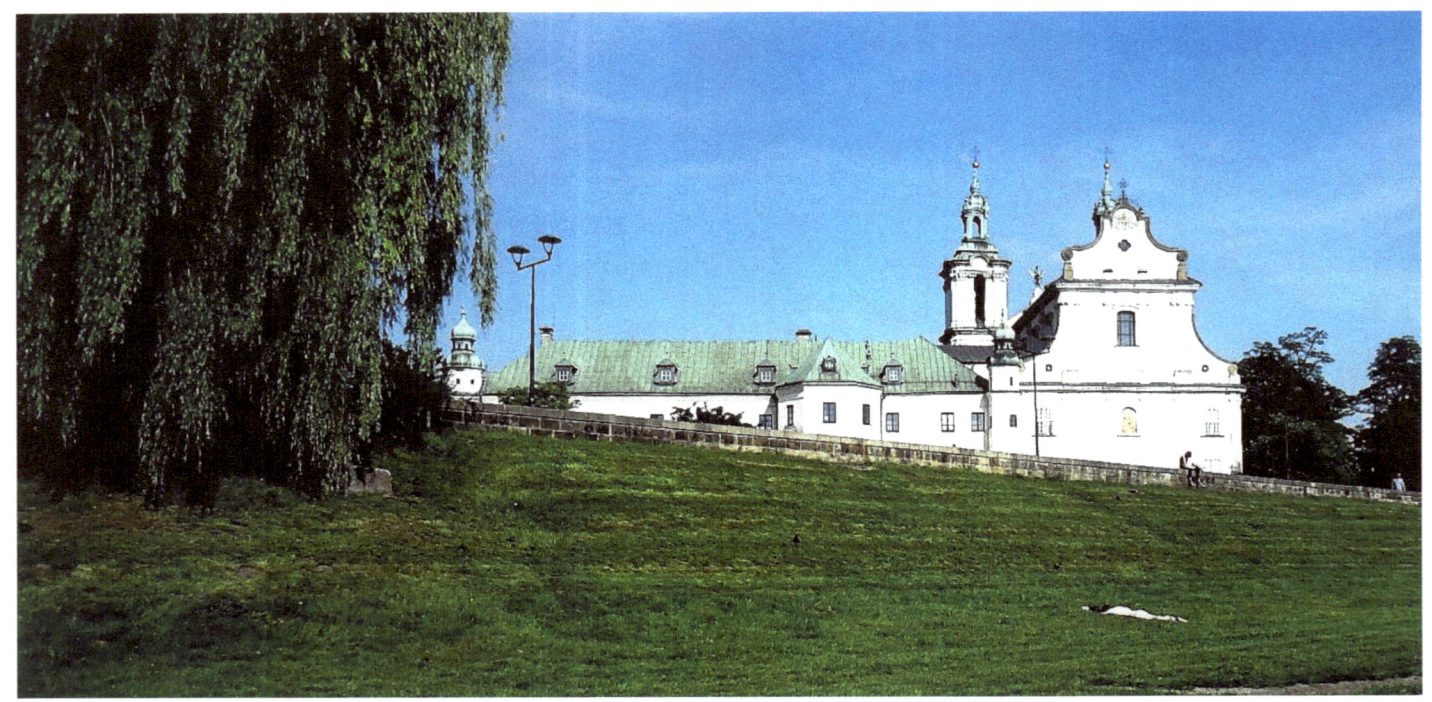

Placki ziemniaczane, potato pancakes. Peel the potatoes and grate them into large pieces, put in a colander and crush them to lose some of their water and transfer in a bowl. Peel and finely chop a white onion, add it to the potatoes, add the egg, chopped parsley, salt, pepper and the necessary flour. Add as much as you need to make the mixture quite dry and full-bodied. Put a pan with high sides on the fire with about 4 tablespoons of oil. Dose the potato mixture with the spoon and pour into the boiling oil. Flatten it in the pan to create rather low pancakes. Let them brown on one side, then turn them around making sure not to break.

Once cooked, place the fritters on absorbent kitchen paper to remove excess grease. Serve the hot potato pancakes, accompanying them to taste with cheese or cucumber or cabbage, beets or even better with mushrooms mixed with a little cream.

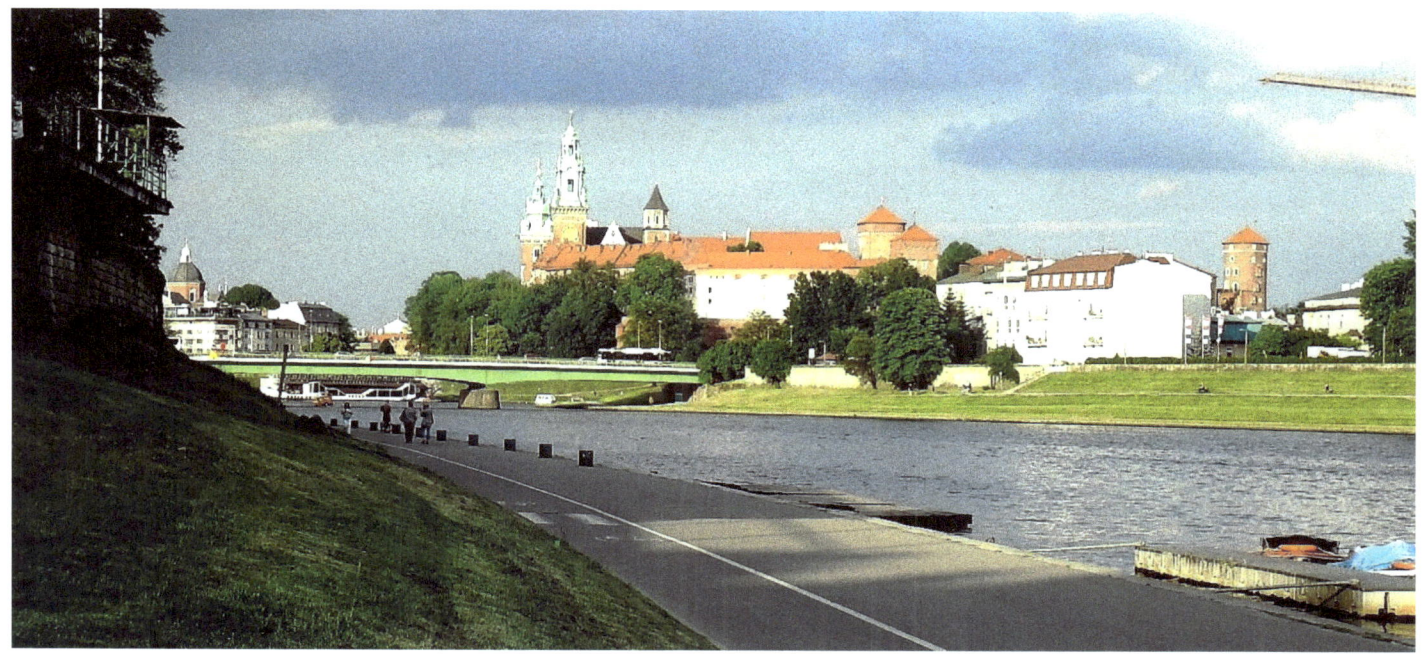

Klops, meatloaf stewed with eggs. Brown an onion in the butter, let it cool and place in a large bowl. Wet the bread with water and add to the bowl. Add a beaten egg to the minced beef with the same amount of pork and mix it all together. Sprinkle a pan of breadcrumbs and put the mixture of meat, stretching to form a rectangle. Place the halves of a hard-boiled egg along the edges, sprinkle with parsley and then roll. Grease an oil pan and heat the oven to 200 degrees. Put the meatloaf in the pan, cover with aluminum foil and leave in the oven for an hour.

Pory, leeks. Wash the leeks well. Put aside most of the green and cook the white parts in plenty of boiling salted water for fifteen minutes, then drain well. Prepare two hard-boiled eggs, crush the egg yolks with a fork and chop the egg whites coarsely. Arrange the leeks on a buttered and hot baking dish. Put the minced eggs on the end of the leeks. Add salt and pepper and sprinkle the dish with a little breadcrumbs and chopped parsley. Pass very briefly in a hot oven. At the last moment, pour in melted butter and lemon juice.

Rosyjska sałatka, Russian salad. Cut the potatoes, carrots, pickled cucumbers, hard-boiled eggs, onion and above all the apple (into small cubes as small as possible), add the peas boiled in salted water and pour the mayonnaise. Add a pinch of mustard. Wanting you can complete the salad with smoked herring or tuna in oil, all in small pieces, cream and dill.

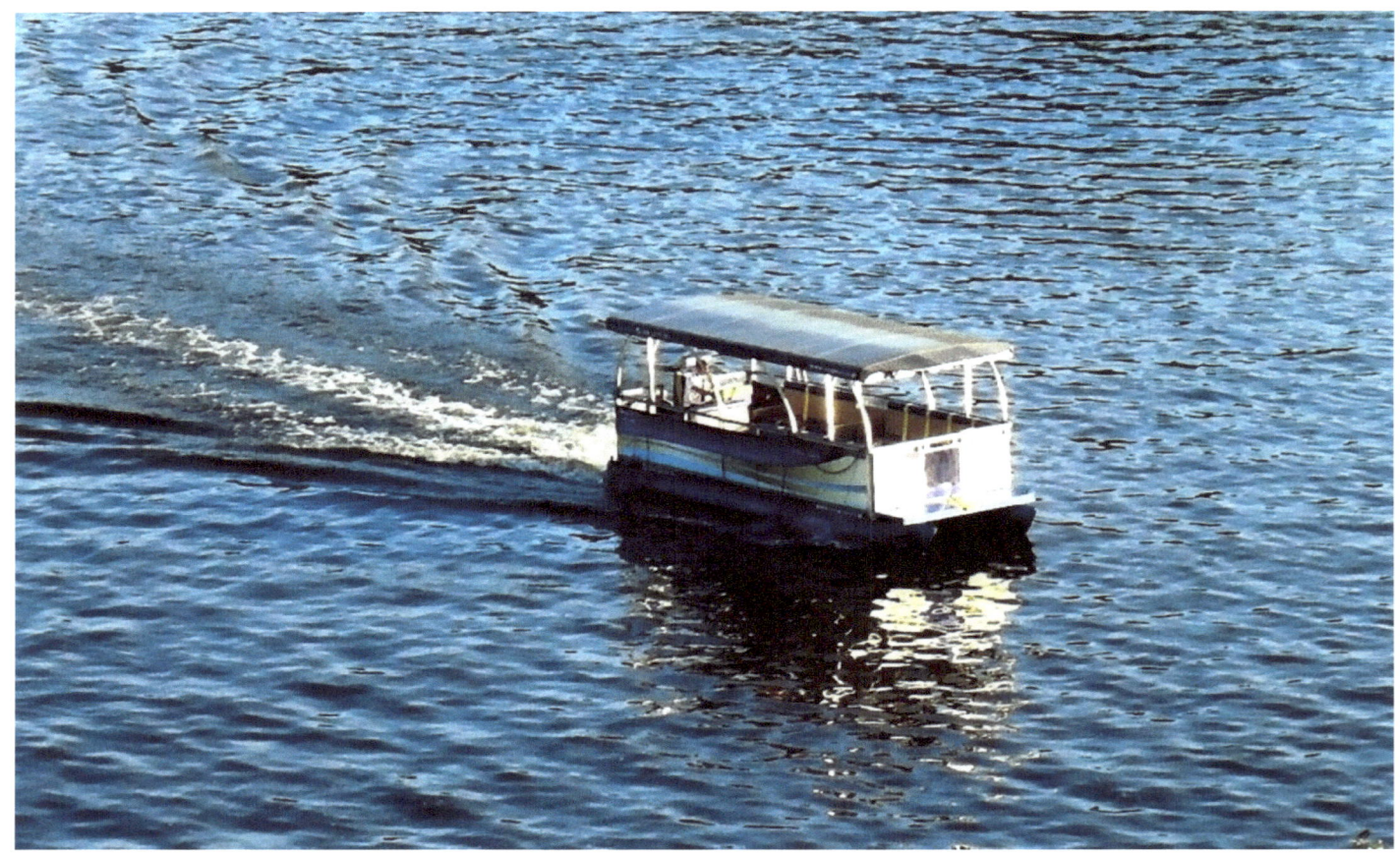

Sałatka ziemniaczana, potato salad. Cook the potatoes with the peel, let them cool, peel and cut into slices. Put them in a salad bowl, add an onion and a sweet and sour cucumber cut into cubes, chives, salt, pepper, vinegar (or lemon) and oil (or mayonnaise or mustard). Add chopped parsley (or dill) and mix. To this basic salad you can add hard-boiled egg cubes, dried tomatoes, olives or other original additions to taste.

Sałatka z porów, jaj i ziemniaków, salad of leeks, eggs and potatoes. Cook the potatoes with the peel, chill, peel, cut into cubes and place them in a salad bowl. Add the leeks cut into small pieces, the hard-boiled eggs, the sweet and sour sliced cucumber and the diced tomato. Mix and add salt, pepper, yogurt (or mayonnaise or mustard) and chopped parsley.

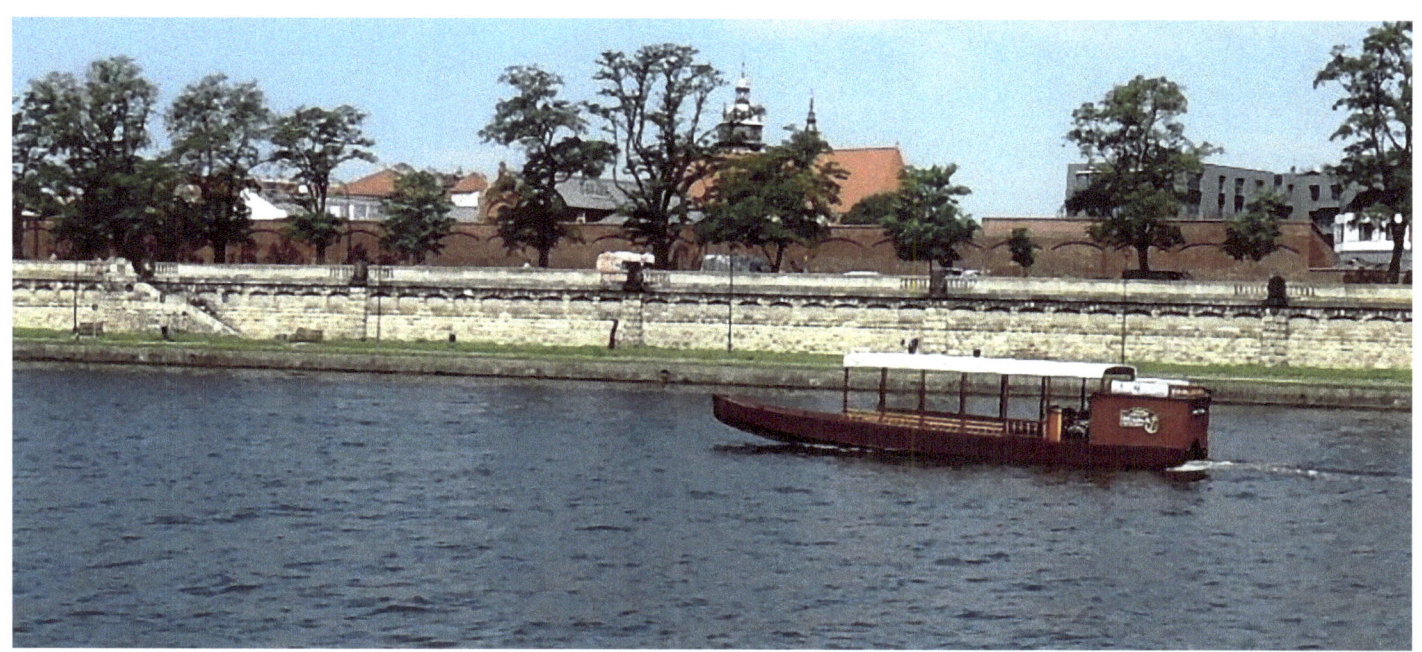

Zapiekanka, wide baguettes cut in half for long (even 50 centimeters) and stuffed with cheese, sautéed white mushrooms and other ingredients to taste creating numerous varieties. Then they are baked until the cheese melts and served with generous ketchup.

Ziemniaki z boczkiem, potatoes with bacon. Cook the potatoes without the peel. When they are cooked remove the water and let it dry a little on the stove (always in the same pot). When they have lost the water, crush them. Fry the onion with the bacon and pour it on the potatoes.

Sernik, ricotta cake. Mix 125g of butter with icing sugar and vanillin, adding one yolk at a time (5 in total)) while stirring. When the dough becomes homogeneous, add one kg of ricotta, potato starch, baking powder, lemon juice, raisin and candied fruit to taste. Whisk the egg whites and add them to the dough. Mix everything gently with a wooden spoon. Pour all into a buttered pan, cook the cake in the oven already hot at 180° for about an hour. Remove it from the oven and let it cool well.

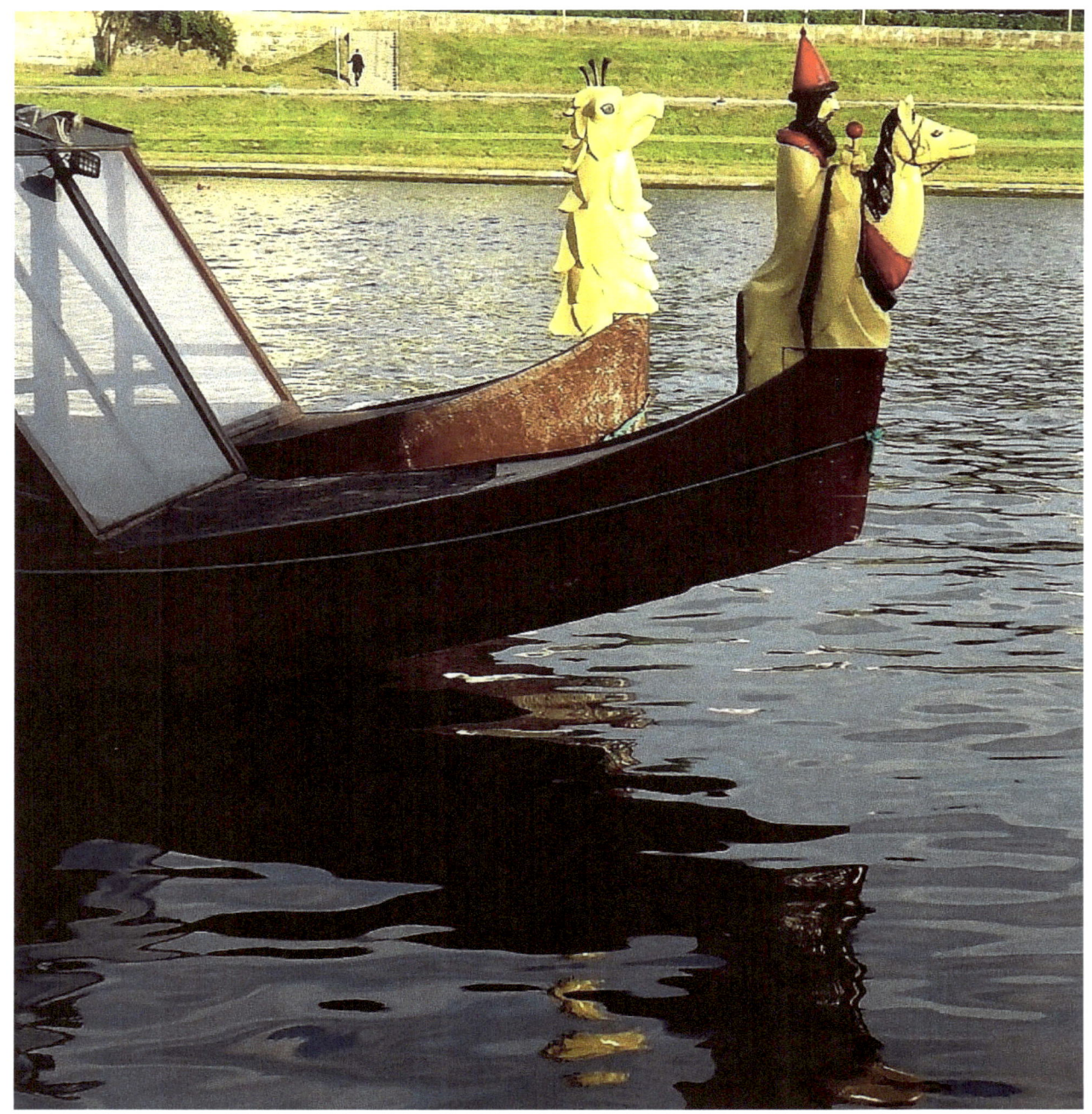

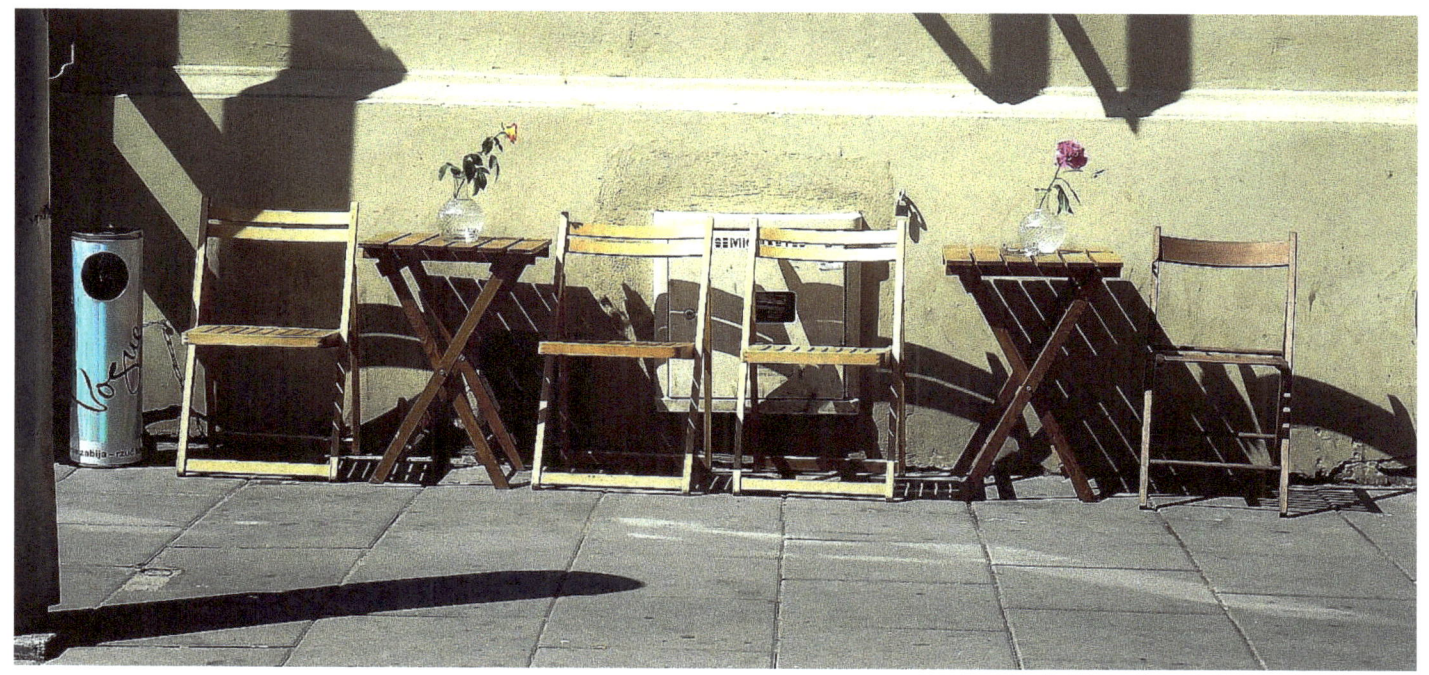

Piernik, Christmas cake. Heat the oven to 175° and cover a 25 cm diameter baking dish with butter and flour. Melt the butter together with the brown sugar in a saucepan. Then add the honey, the plum jam, the spices for the *piernik* (cinnamon, ginger, cloves, star anise, cardamom and pepper) and heat for a few minutes. Remove the saucepan from the heat, let the butter cool and add the bicarbonate, the soluble barley, a cup of milk and 2 beaten eggs. Stir energetically for a few minutes as the mixture mixes well. Add the sifted flour and mix well. Put the mixture in the pan and bake for 50 minutes. When cooked, pull out and let it cool. Cut the cake in half and spread the plum jam between the two halves. For the garnish heat the cream in a saucepan, add a tablespoon of soluble barley and stir. When the barley has melted, add and melt the chocolate breaked into pieces. Spread the garnish over the *piernik*, wait for it solidifies and serve.

Chrust, cake of the eve of the Ash-Wednesday. Mix the softened butter, the egg yolks, the icing sugar and the alcohol or vinegar, slowly adding the flour until it forms a dough. Continue to beat and knead the mixture for 15 minutes. Put it in a bowl, cover and let it rest in a cool place for an hour. Roll out the dough until you get a very thin sheet. Cut it into strips of 4x14 cm, make an incision in the middle of each strip and let there pass one of two ends. Fry them in a pan with the bacon or oil. Fry 4-5 strips at a time by turning them on both sides. Remove from the oil and place them on a sheet of absorbent paper. Sprinkle with plenty of powdered sugar.

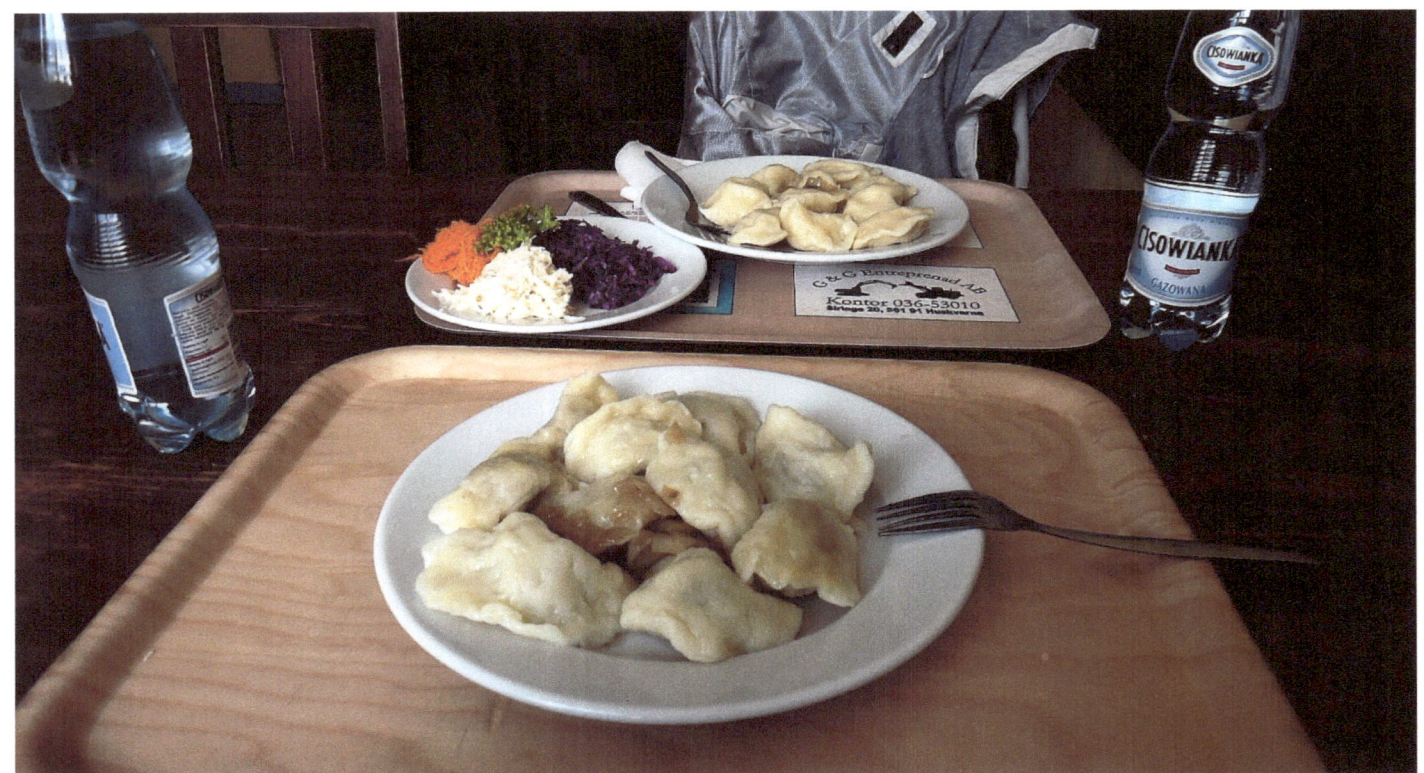

Makowiec, Christmas cake with poppy seeds. Dissolve 50g of yeast in milk, add a tablespoon of sugar and flour in a quantity to form a dense mixture and let it rest. Then add the remaining flour, 5 egg yolks, 100g of sugar, the essence of vanilla and a pinch of salt, working with a wooden spoon. Add 150g of lukewarm butter dissolved with oil and let it rest. Add 500g of poppy seeds after washing them, made to bolil in water and passed 3 times in the meat grinder. Add the vanilla sugar and heat over low heat, stirring well. When all the sugar has melted add the fried orange peel, the vanilla sugar and any raisins. With the dough ready form a pastry, cover it with the poppy seeds and roll it up. Transfer it to an elongated mold, covered with aluminum foil and left to rise in a warm place. When the mass has grown, put the mold in the oven at 160°. When cooked, let it cool and sprinkle with icing sugar.

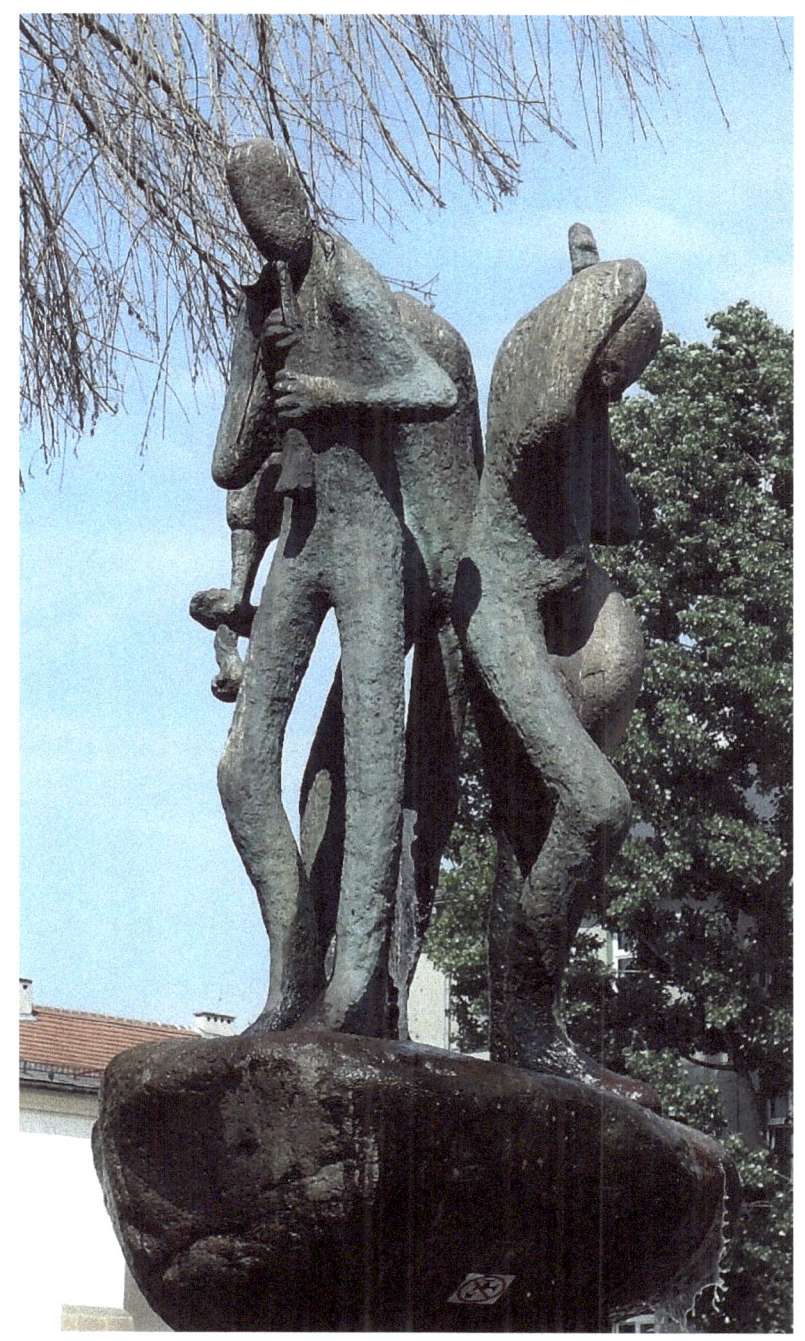

59

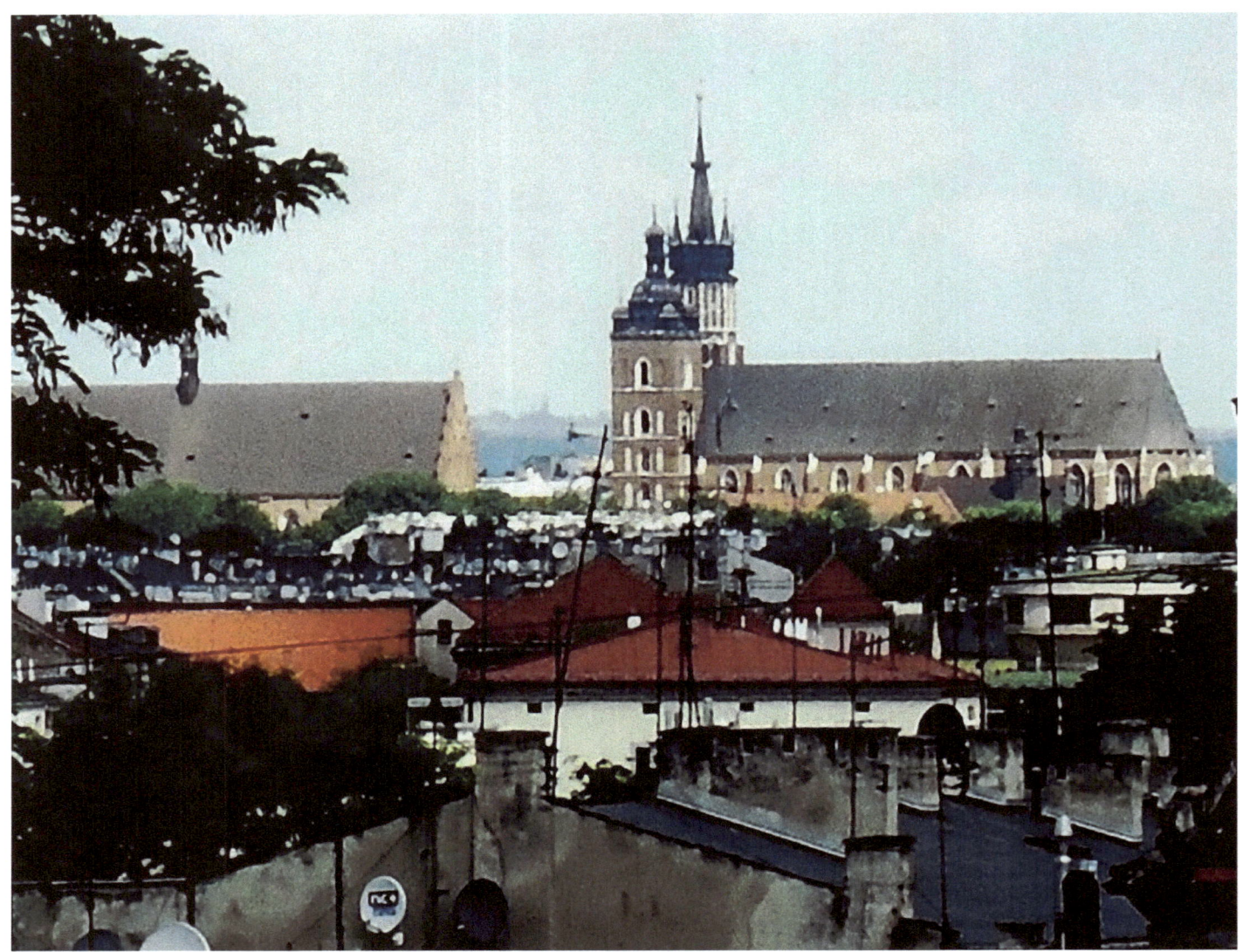

Grog z miodem, honey grog. Heat the tea infusion with buckwheat honey, add the cinnamon and the open vanilla pod. Crush the cloves and peppercorns well and immerse them in the liquid together with the grated nutmeg. Let simmer for 15 minutes, then pour the vodka and flavor with the grated lemon peel. Let everything well covered for 10 minutes over a low flame. Before serving, filter the grog through a strainer and pour it into the previously heated glasses.

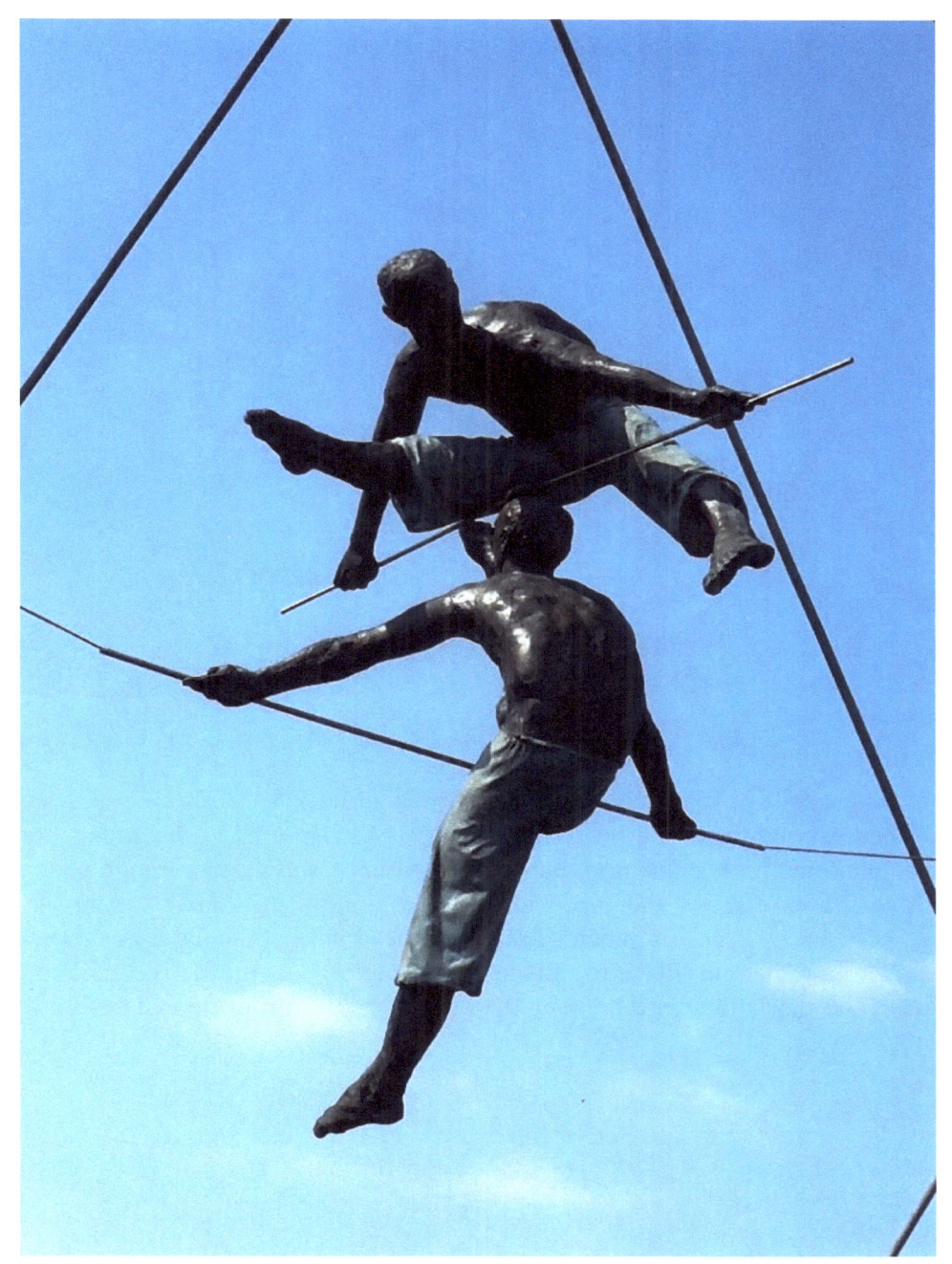

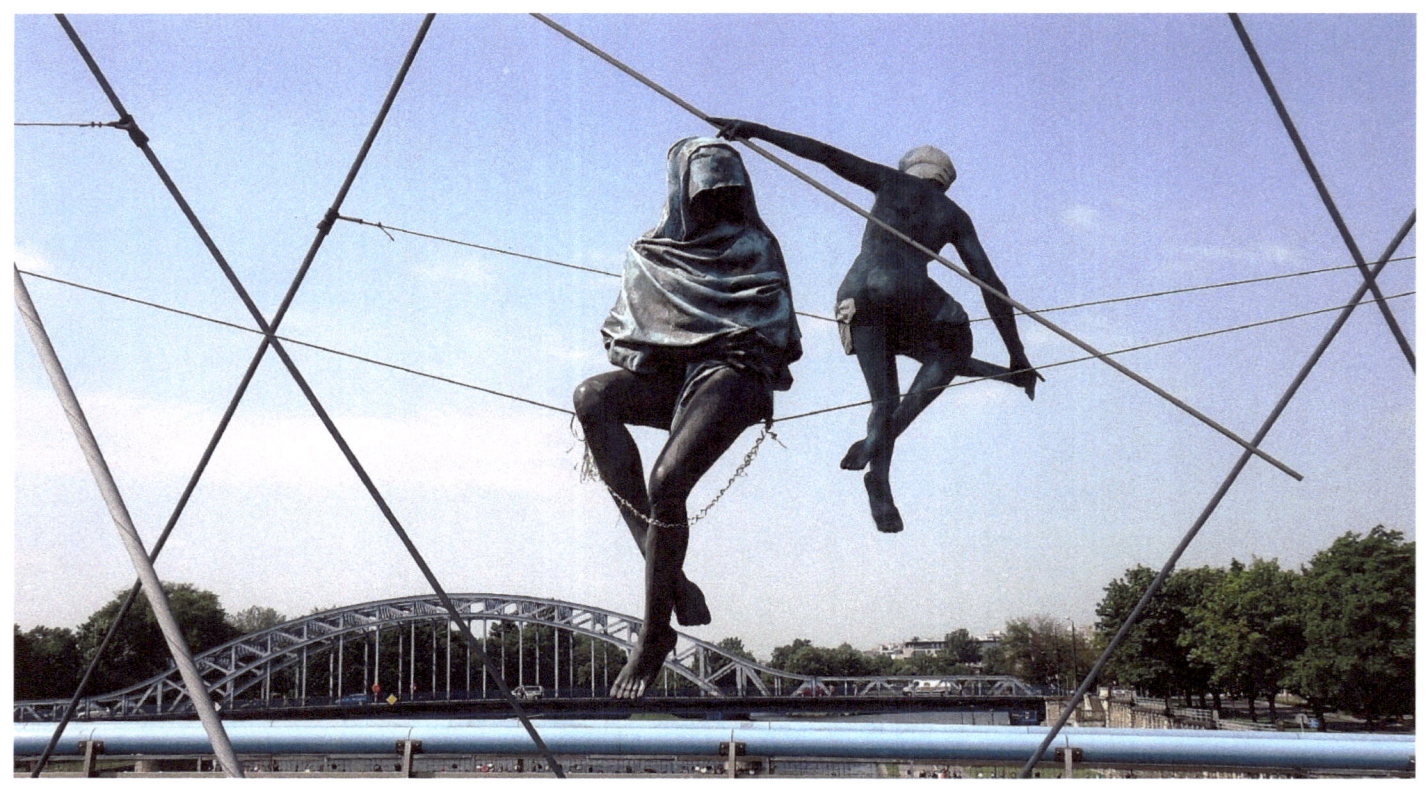

Polski strudel, Polish strudel. Stuffing: boil the milk, slowly add a kilo of poppy seeds, cook for 5 minutes, stirring constantly, then remove from the heat and let it rest. Mix in a bowl the sugar, breadcrumbs, honey, raisins, chopped walnuts, pine nuts, cinnamon, butter, orange juice and grated orange peel. Add everything to the mixture of milk and poppy seeds and mix well. For the dough: in a bowl put the flour, milk, sugar, 2 eggs, grated orange peel, butter, yeast, a pinch of salt and knead until obtaining a homogeneous mixture. Roll out the dough and make a rectangle. Place the filling in the center and roll the rectangle on itself, sealing the sides well. Brush with the egg yolk, sprinkle over the poppy seeds kept aside and cook in preheated oven at 180° for about 50 minutes.

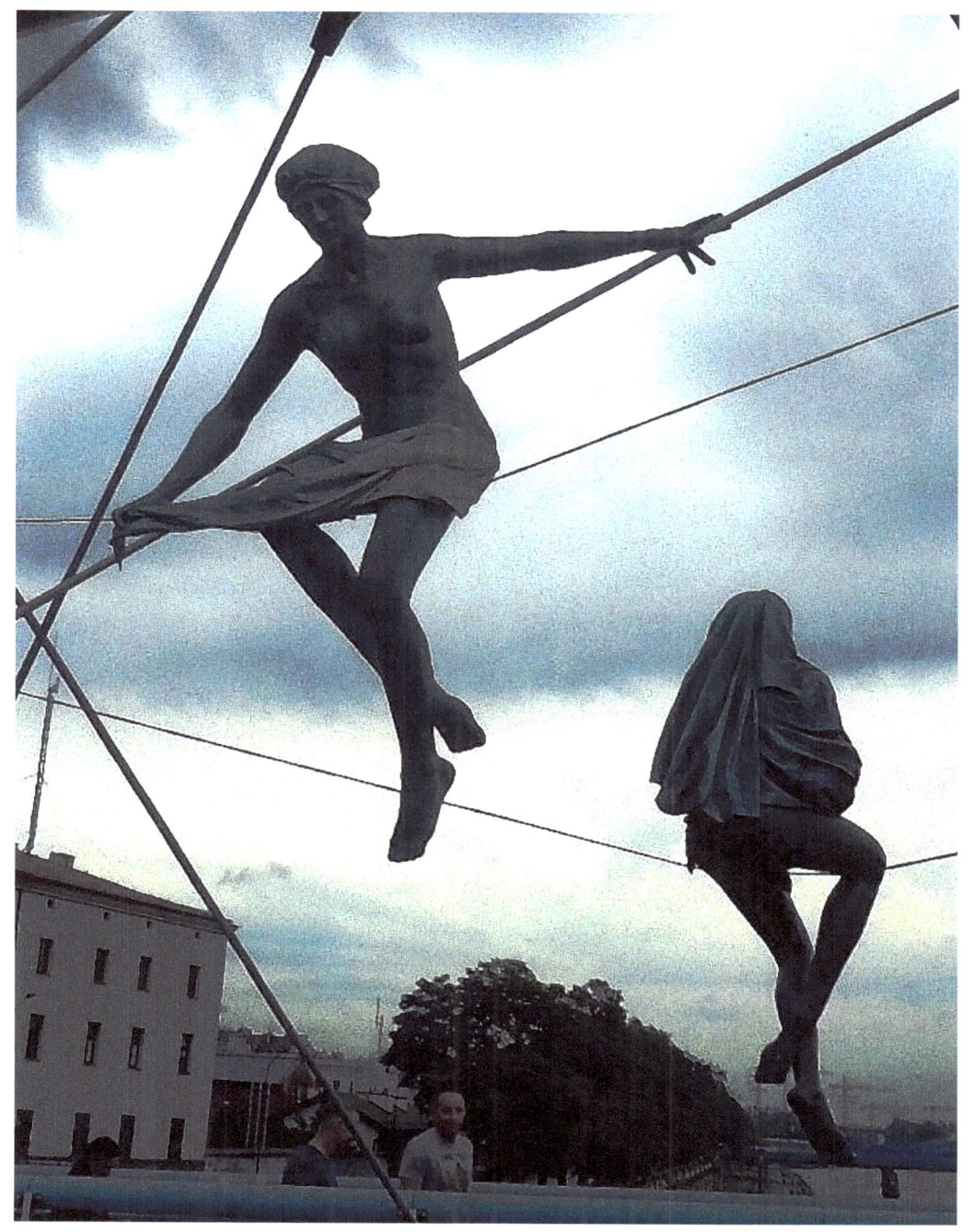

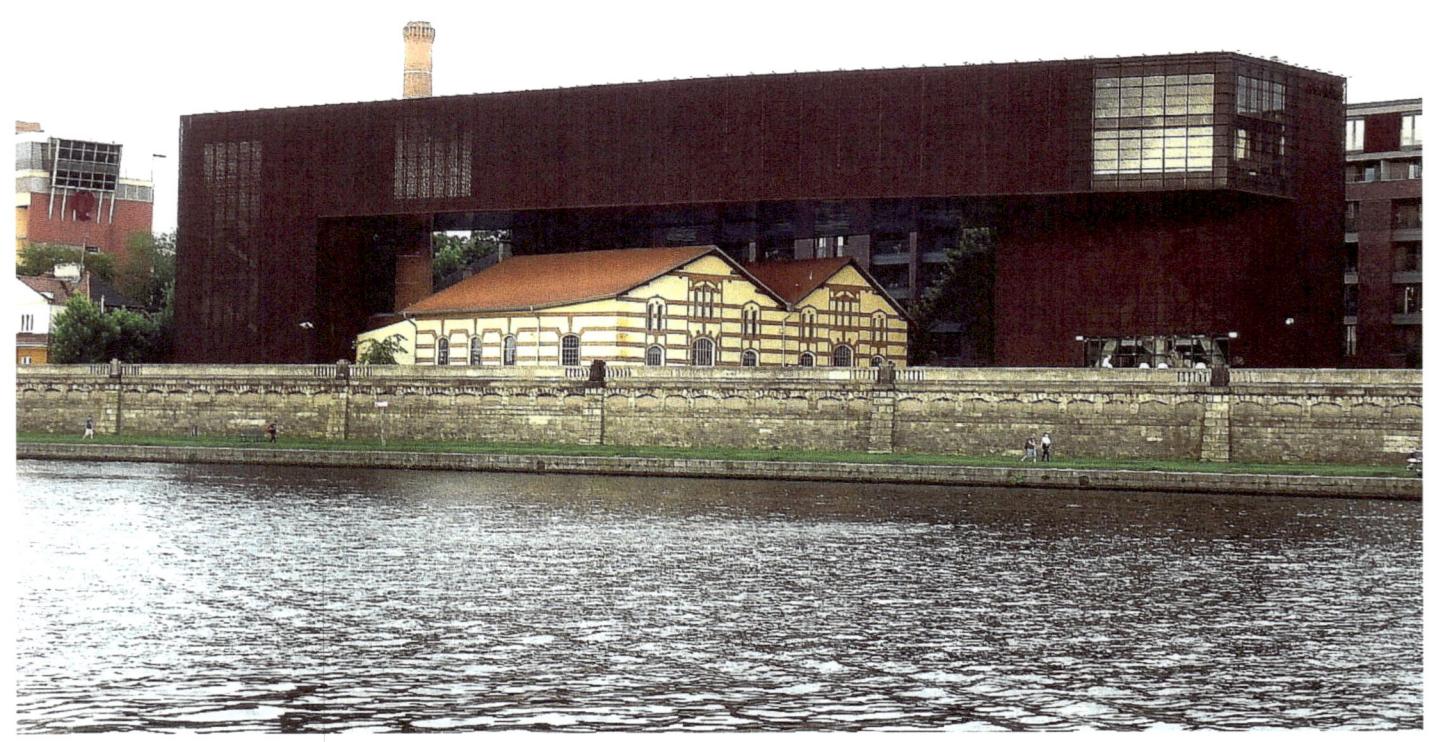

Mazurek, cake for Easter. Shortcrust pastry: mix the softened butter in a bowl and cut into small pieces with the flour and powdered sugar. Add milk, egg, a pinch of salt and quickly work the dough. Obtained a smooth and compact dough, let it rest in the refrigerator for 30 minutes. Preheat the oven to 220°. Filling: mix other softened butter with sugar, 100g of bitter cocoa and 2 egg yolks. Put in the flour always mixing the dough, so as not to form lumps.

Remove the shortcrust pastry from the fridge and roll it into a mold, prick the surface with a fork and let it cook in white for 20 minutes. Check the cooking frequently to make sure that the pasta is well cooked. While cooking, prepare the garnish by mixing the ingredients, leaving aside the almonds. Wanting you can also add a tablespoon of rum. Pour the garnish into the bottom of the dough, add the almonds and let it cool for an hour in the fridge. You can also add candied orange peel.

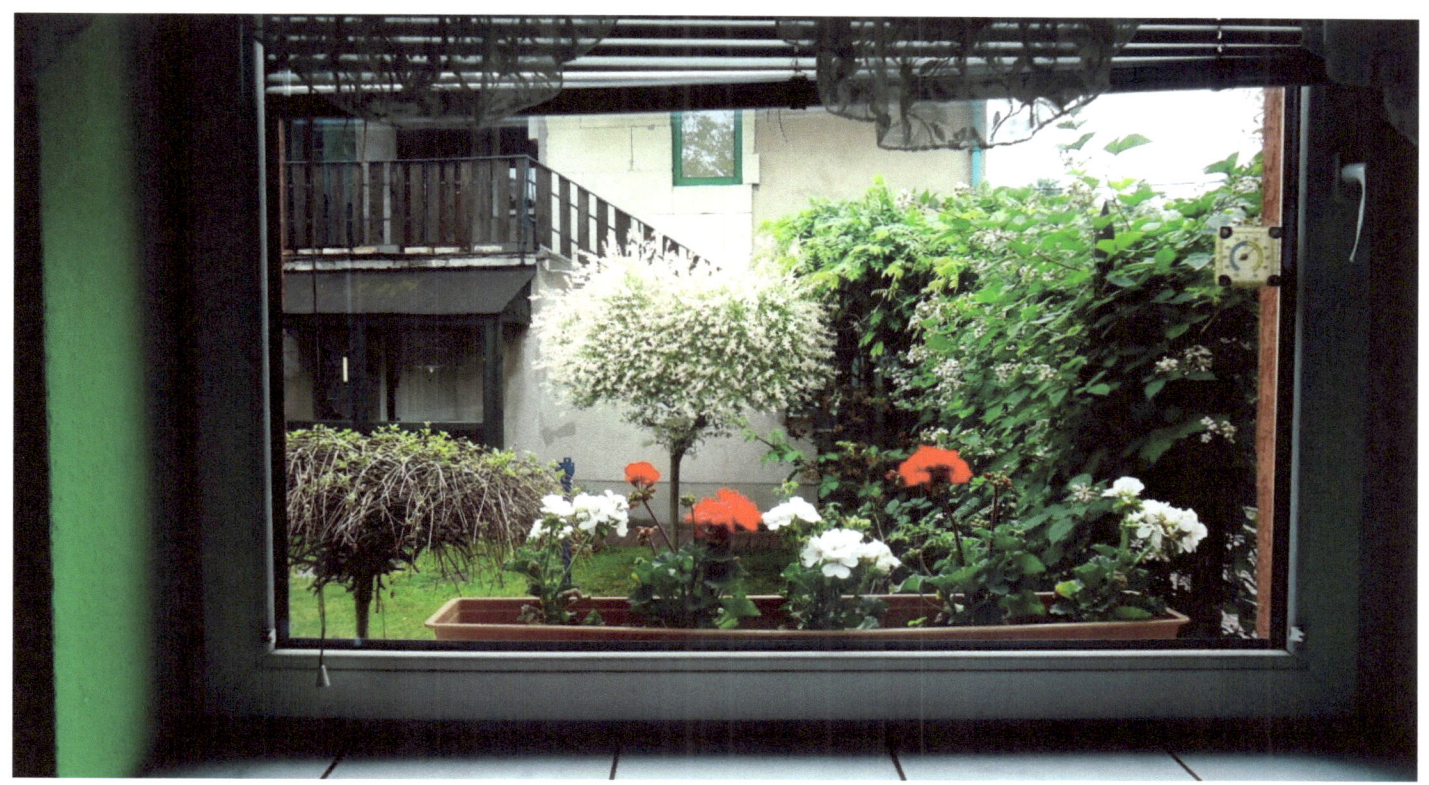

Babka polska, sweet of the Easter tradition. Soften 200g of butter at room temperature and in the meantime prepare the other ingredients: sieve 150g of flour, 100g of potato starch and a sachet of baking powder. Grease a pan and then sprinkle with breadcrumbs. Work the softened butter with 200g of powdered sugar until you obtain a soft and fluffy mixture, then add four egg yolks, flour and starch, a few drops of almond essence, sour cream, grated peel and the juice of a lemon and raisins.

Beat the egg whites until stiff and add them to the dough, mixing from top to bottom gently to avoid disassembling them. Quickly transfer the mixture into the cake tin, which must be placed in a pre-heated oven at 180°. Cook for about 40 minutes and then let it cool. Once cold, transfer the babka to a serving dish and decorate with icing sugar or other Easter-themed decorations.

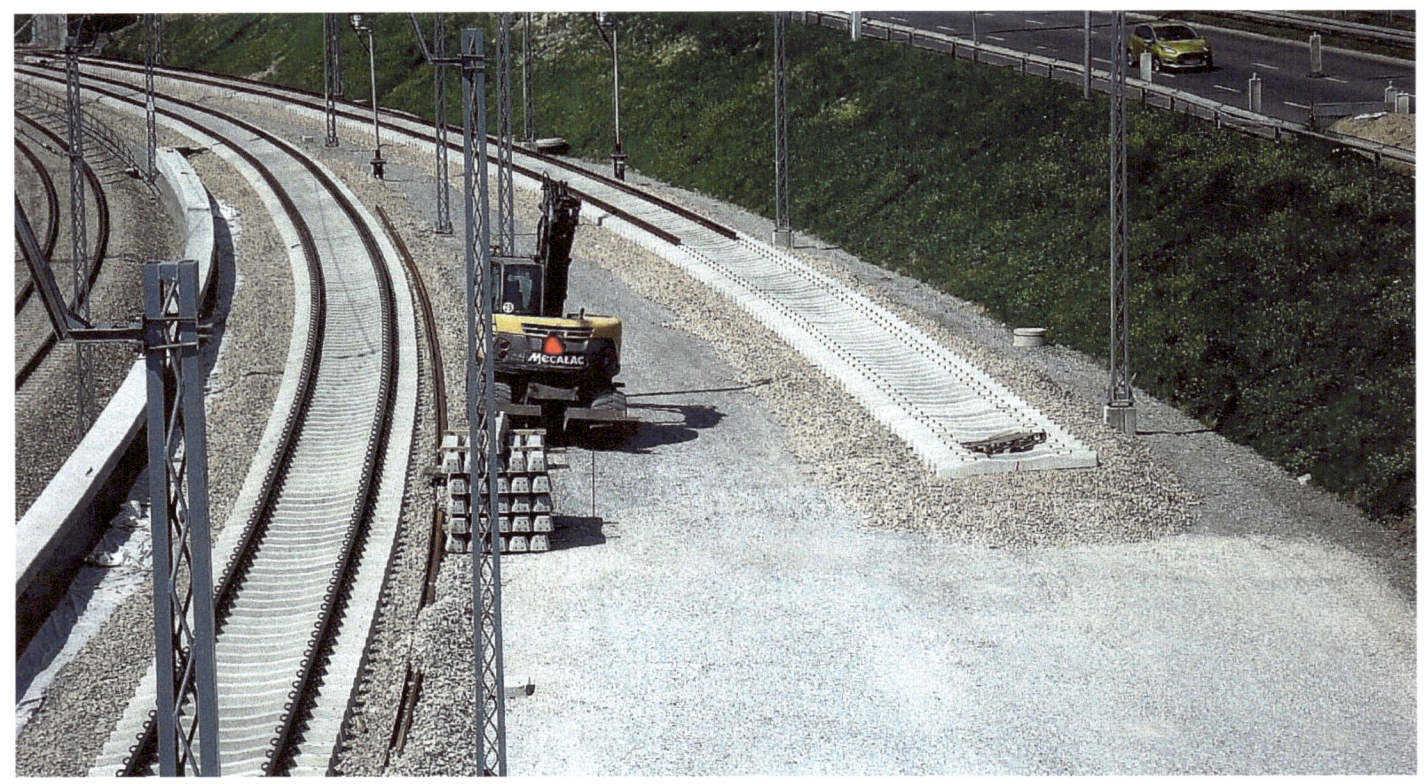

Czekoladowa babka, chocolate babka. Melt crumbled brewer's yeast in lukewarm water in a bowl. Pour into the planetary 260g of manitoba flour and 260g of 00 flour, the water with the yeast, the sugar, 2 eggs and the yolk already beaten and the grated rind of a lemon. Start working with the kneading hook and gradually add 140g of soft butter into small pieces and the salt up. Continue to work the dough until you get a well-mixed dough, which must be very soft and elastic, but not sticky. Take the dough, form a sphere and place it in a narrow, high bowl. Cover with a kitchen towel or foil and leave to rise until doubled.

Stuffing: in a bowl melt the chocolate with the butter and sugar and when they are melted, add the cocoa and mix well. Let it cool, then let it harden in the refrigerator for 10 minutes. It is necessary to obtain a slightly firmer consistency than that of a spreadable cream. Take back the leavened dough and divide it into two parts. Spread both in a rectangle as long as the mold you use for cooking, spread the filling and roll it being careful not to let the filling out. Cut the rolls in half leaving one end attached, wrap the two parts together to form a interlacement so that the cut part always remains upwards…

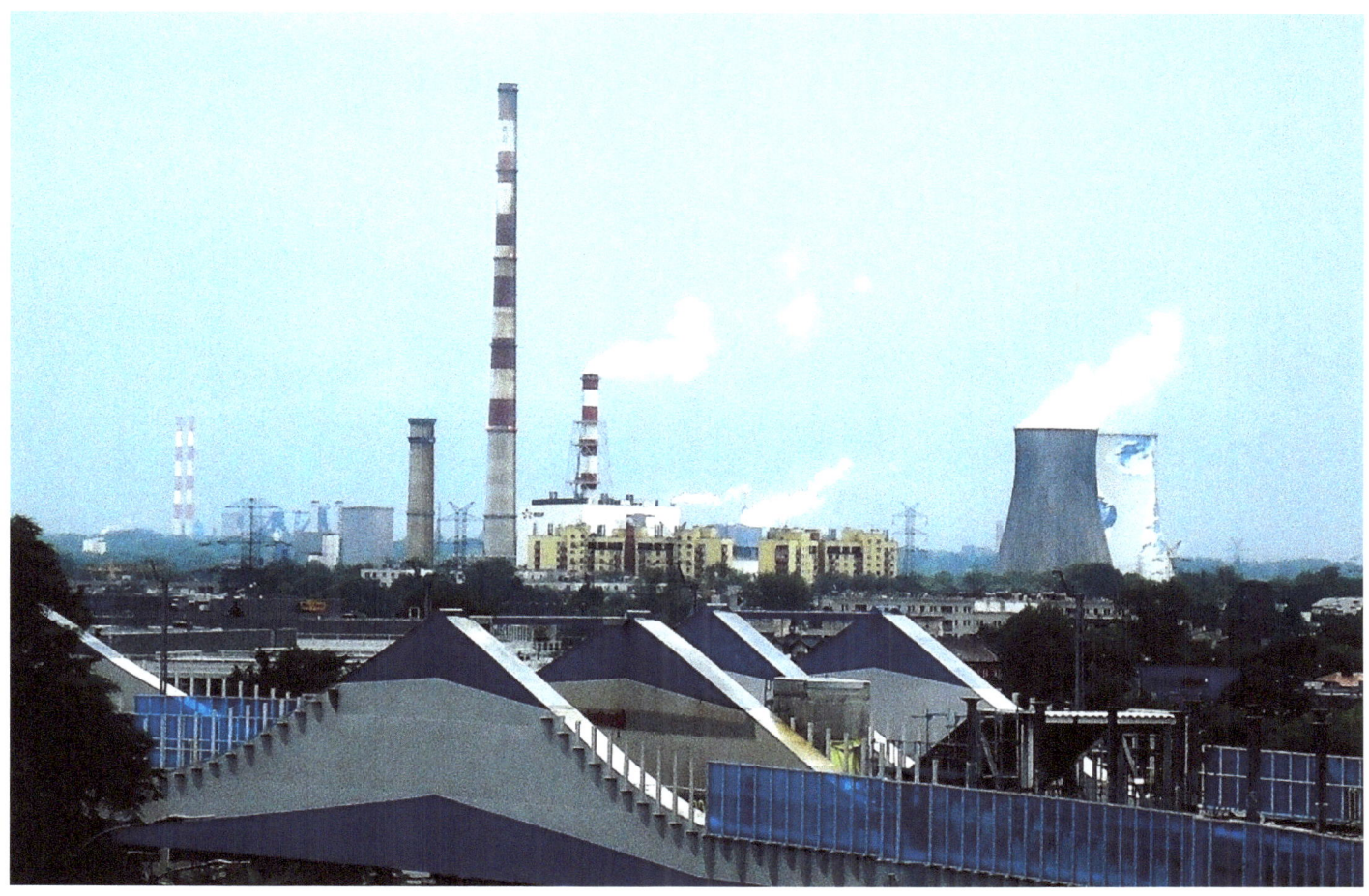

…In case the pasta is too soft, put the rolls in the fridge for half an hour to harden, before cutting them. Put the braids made inside two buttered molds, cover with a cloth and let the dough double. Heat the oven to 180° and bake the babka for 40 minutes. If the surface gets too dark, cover it with aluminum foil. In a saucepan put the remaining sugar and add the water, bring to a boil and cook 4-5 minutes, then let it cool completely. Remove the cake and pour over the frosting. Before removing the babka from the mold let it cool.

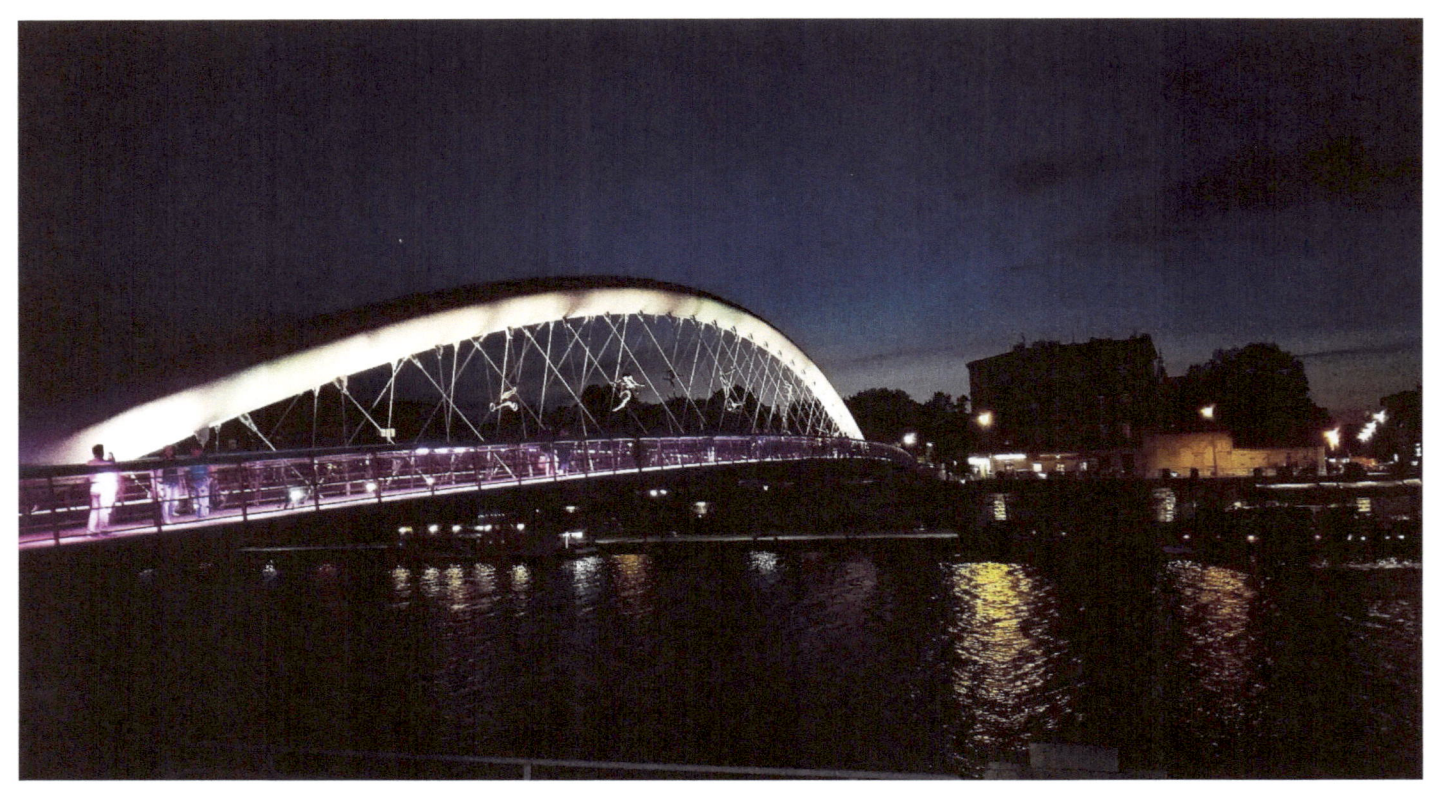

www.ingramcontent.com/pod-product-compliance
Lightning Source LLC
Chambersburg PA
CBHW041501280526
45792CB00004B/1093